Dear Patsy,

Next time they send you off
to some exotic land, check
it out in this little book!

Merry Christmas,
Donna

The

TRAVELING

CURMUDGEON

BOOKS BY JON WINOKUR

A Curmudgeon's Garden of Love

Advice to Writers

Fathers

Friendly Advice

Happy Motoring (with Norrie Epstein)

How to Win at Golf Without Actually Playing Well

Je Ne Sais What?

Mondo Canine

The Portable Curmudgeon

The Portable Curmudgeon Redux

The Rich Are Different

True Confessions

Writers on Writing

Zen to Go

The

TRAVELING CURMUDGEON

IRREVERENT NOTES, QUOTES, AND ANECDOTES
ON DISMAL DESTINATIONS, EXCESS BAGGAGE,
THE FULL UPRIGHT POSITION,
AND OTHER REASONS NOT TO GO THERE

Compiled and Edited by

JON WINOKUR

SASQUATCH BOOKS
SEATTLE

For JG

Printed in Canada
Published by Sasquatch Books
Distributed by Publishers Group West
10 09 08 07 06 05 04   6 5 4 3 2

Cover and interior design: Kate Basart
Cover illustration: Patrick Moriarty
Copy editor: Amy Smith Bell

Library of Congress Cataloging in Publication Data
The traveling curmudgeon : irreverent notes, quotes, and
anecdotes on dismal destinations, excess baggage, the full upright position, and
other reasons not to go there / compiled and edited by Jon Winokur.
        p.   cm
Includes index
ISBN 1-57061-389-3
1. Travel—Quotations, maxims, etc. 2. Travel—Anecdotes. I. Winokur, Jon.

PN6084.T7T68 2003
910—dc21   2003045610

Sasquatch Books
119 South Main Street, Suite 400
Seattle, WA 98104
206/467-4300
www.sasquatchbooks.com
books@sasquatchbooks.com

cur•mud•geon \k∂r'm∂j-∂n\ **n** [origin unknown]

1 archaic: a crusty, ill-tempered, churlish old man

2 modern: anyone who hates hypocrisy and pretense and has the temerity to say so; anyone with the habit of pointing out unpleasant facts in an engaging and humorous manner

There has been, of late, a strange turn in travelers to be displeased.

SAMUEL JOHNSON

CONTENTS

INTRODUCTION

Travel writing is the literature of complaint, and bad trips have always been good material, from *The Odyssey* to *Robinson Crusoe,* Marco Polo to Mark Twain, Graham Greene to Bill Bryson. No one wants to read about a halcyon voyage on glassy seas, a routine flight in first class aboard a half-empty 747, a glorious stay at a four-star hotel with sumptuous food and fabulous service. Comfort and luxury are forgettable. Misery is memorable. "The worst trips make the best reading," writes Paul Theroux, who proves it in book after book. "Writing about good times is just boasting," he says. "They want to hear about the hitches."

We love travel horror stories. There are now websites with postings about lost reservations, missed connections, one-way round-trips, runway delays (some so long that the plane can't take off without refueling), exorbitant prices, ruined honeymoons, hotels from hell, inedible food, unsanitary conditions, etc., etc., etc., ad—yes—nauseam.

A bad trip is guaranteed to rivet listeners at a party. Except that they can't wait for you to finish so they can tell you about their own disasters. It's a form of snobbery. Those who survive bad trips are just a tad smug: "Look what I endured," they brag, as they detail every indignity. "But I came through, by golly, because I love to travel!" They assume one can't be "cultivated" without travel, and they take pride in their determination to "broaden" themselves in the face of adversity.

But *have* they broadened themselves? What have they learned except how to operate the shutter delay, how much to tip the concierge, or how to file a lost luggage claim? What have they seen except the usual tourist traps on an increasingly beaten track around an ever more crowded and homogenized world?

These intrepids insist that there's no substitute for travel, even if you have to suffer. They believe that there's no pleasure without pain, so you might as well embrace the pain. They maintain that it's all worth the frustration, the discomfort, even the occasional danger.

On the contrary. Travel isn't what it used to be, if it ever was. Endless security checks, jet lag, homesickness, loneliness, strange food, unpleasant seat mates, the shocking realization that the U.S. Constitution has no force outside the United States—the hardships are definitely *not* worth the rewards.

"Travel" derives from *travail,* French for "arduous toil." Exactly. Travel is work. Trace the etymology back even further and you find the Latin word for torture.

Why travel when you can experience almost anything in the world vicariously, in the comfort of your own home? With the advent of streaming video, HDTV, and, sooner or later, virtual reality—not to mention a rich body of travel literature—why go anywhere? Let someone else do the work while you reap the rewards without the hassle and risk.

Hence this volume, a catalog of "hitches," a paean to the joys of Not Going, an antitravel book, to explode the myth that travel is some sort of cultural hygiene necessary for mental or spiritual health. It will liberate you, dear reader, from the tyranny of the travel/industrial complex, and, I trust, persuade you to make all your journeys imaginary.

So sit back, kick off your slippers, and unfasten your seat belt: It's going to be a comfy ride.

J.W.
Pacific Palisades

DON'T GO THERE

Addis Ababa

Breathing and occasional heart attacks caused by the rarefied air are the only discomforts during the first few days.

LADISLAS FARAGO

Africa

Life in Africa is nasty, British, and short.

PAUL THEROUX

It is not the fully conscious mind which chooses West Africa in preference to Switzerland.

GRAHAM GREENE

Akron

Akron, Ohio, is the only place in the world people from Cleveland are entitled to make fun of.

BARRY CRIMMINS

[Suggested motto:] Preferable to Youngstown.

CALVIN TRILLIN

Alaska

Alaska was originally a large place located way the hell up past Canada, but this proved to be highly inconvenient for mapmakers, who in 1873 voted to make it smaller and put it in a little box next to Hawaii right off the coast of California, which is where it is today.

DAVE BARRY

Alaska represents the ultimate time-activity ratio nightmare: Nothing to do and twenty-two hours of daylight in which not to do it.

MARK LAWSON

America

America is the only nation in history which miraculously has gone directly from barbarism to degeneration without the usual interval of civilization.

GEORGES CLEMENCEAU

I have never been able to look upon America as young and vital, but rather as prematurely old, as a fruit which rotted before it had a chance to ripen. The word which gives the key to the national vice is waste.

HENRY MILLER

Perhaps, after all, America never has been discovered. I myself would say that it had merely been detected.

OSCAR WILDE

An asylum for the sane would be empty in America.

GEORGE BERNARD SHAW

American: Wonderful man, Columbus.
Oscar Wilde: Why?
American: He discovered America.
Wilde: Oh no, it had been discovered before, but it had always been hushed up.

In our country we have those three unspeakably precious things: freedom of speech, freedom of conscience, and the prudence never to practice either.
MARK TWAIN

Any man who could live in America is insane.
EZRA POUND

The civilization whose absence drove Henry James to Europe.
GORE VIDAL

In America sex is an obsession, in other parts of the world it is a fact.
MARLENE DIETRICH

Every time Europe looks across the Atlantic to see the American eagle, it observes only the rear end of an ostrich.
AMBROSE BIERCE

In modern America, anyone who attempts to write satirically about the events of the day finds it difficult to concoct a situation so bizarre that it may not actually come to pass while the article is still on the presses.
CALVIN TRILLIN

America . . . just a nation of two hundred million used car salesmen
with all the money we need to buy guns and no qualms about killing anybody
else in the world who tries to make us uncomfortable.

HUNTER S. THOMPSON

The land of the dull and the home of the literal.

GORE VIDAL

In America, through pressure of conformity, there is freedom of choice,
but nothing to choose from.

PETER USTINOV

The discovery of America was the occasion of the greatest outburst
of cruelty and reckless greed known in history.

JOSEPH CONRAD

America is the greatest of opportunities and the worst of influences.

GEORGE SANTAYANA

STATE MOTTOES WE'D LIKE TO SEE

Rhode Island: Land of Obscurity
Oklahoma: The Recruiting Violations State
Minnesota: Too Damn Cold
Wisconsin: Eat Cheese or Die
California: Freeway Congestion with Occasional Gunfire
New Jersey: Armpit of the Nation
North Dakota: Incredibly Boring
Nebraska: More Interesting Than North Dakota
New York: We're Not Arrogant, We're Just Better Than You

MOLLY IVINS

My country, 'tis of thee
Sweet land of felony
Of thee I sing
Land where my father fried
Young witches and applied
Whips to the Quakers hide
And made him spring.
AMBROSE BIERCE

America is still a government of the naive, by the naive,
and for the naive. He who does not know this, nor relish it, has no
inkling of the nature of this country.
CHRISTOPHER MORLEY

A country with thirty religions and only one sauce.
TALLEYRAND

America is a country no one should go to for the first time.
JAWAHARLAL NEHRU

America is a mistake, a giant mistake!
SIGMUND FREUD

American cities are like badger holes, ringed with trash—
all of them—surrounded by piles of rusting automobiles,
and almost smothered with rubbish.
JOHN STEINBECK

The big cities of America are becoming Third-World countries.
NORA EPHRON

Arkansas

I know New Yorkers who have been to Cochin, China, Kafristan,
Somaliland, and West Virginia, but not one who has ever penetrated
the miasmic jungle of Arkansas.

H. L. MENCKEN

Happy is the state that has not history—and Arkansas has none.
It was not founded by a pious Aeneas, nor fought over by Hannibals and
Scipios. It just grew up out of seepage.

C. L. EDSON

I didn't make Arkansas the butt of ridicule. God did.

H. L. MENCKEN

Atlanta

Atlanta is what a quarter of a million Confederate soldiers died to prevent.

JOHN SHELTON REED

Atlantic Ocean

Disappointing.

OSCAR WILDE

Australia

Australia, *n.* A country lying in the South Sea whose industrial and
commercial development has been unspeakably retarded by an unfortunate
dispute among geographers as to whether it is a continent or an island.

AMBROSE BIERCE

Australia is an outdoor country. People only go inside to use the toilet.
And that's only a recent development.

BARRY HUMPHRIES

If you want to know what it is to feel the "correct" social world
fizzle to nothing, you should come to Australia.

D. H. LAWRENCE

Canada with an accent and a few cute phrases.

JOEL STEIN

It's so empty and featureless, like a newspaper that has been
entirely censored. We used to drive for miles, always expecting that
round the next corner there would be something to look at,
and there never was. That's the charm of Australia.

ROBERT MORLEY

There are many non-intellectual countries;
Australia is one of the few anti-intellectual ones.

GEORGE MIKES

Australia is less like a foreign country than anywhere else I've been.
It has the same toothpastes we do, the same food, the same cars. It can't
even produce indigenous television. I saw an even more vapid version of Matt
Lauer on Australia's own *Today* show and a better-looking Mike Wallace on a
local version of *60 Minutes*. Unfortunately, the episode I saw of *Caroline in
the City* was the real American version of *Caroline in the City*.

JOEL STEIN

Bali

It's not the heat [in Bali], it's the humidity. The sheets on the bed that you
don't sleep in are soaking wet when you wake up in the morning. The fattest
James Michener paperback curls into a soggy cylinder on the nightstand.
Even in an air-conditioned room, your pillowcase can be mistaken for the
natural habitat of the Balinese gecko, as I discovered after turning in my
first night on the island. Come daytime, it really gets humid.

STEVE RUSHIN

Belfast

There is a story that when incoming jets throttle back for the
approach to Belfast's Aldergrove Airport, the pilots tell their passengers
to put their watches back to local time—1690.

RUSSELL MILLER

Belgium

Belgium is known affectionately to the French as "the gateway to Germany"
and just as affectionately to the Germans as "the gateway to France."

TONY HENDRA

Northern Ireland run by the Swiss.

MARK LAWSON

Belize

One of the first things that strike the newcomer to Belize who has seen anything of life in the West Indies is the mysterious absence of anything that might come under the heading of having a good time.

NORMAN LEWIS

Bermuda

In the symphony of life, Bermuda is a three-bar rest.

FRED ALLEN

Beverly Hills

If you stay in Beverly Hills too long you become a Mercedes.

ROBERT REDFORD

Once I was coming down a street in Beverly Hills and I saw a Cadillac about a block long, and out of the side window was a wonderfully slinky mink, and an arm, and at the end of the arm a hand in a white suede glove wrinkled around the wrist, and in the hand was a bagel with a bite out of it.

DOROTHY PARKER

Beverly Hills is very exclusive. For instance, their fire department won't make house calls.

MORT SAHL

Bombay

The nightlife of Bombay is roughly on par with that of Schwenksville, Pennsylvania.

S. J. PERELMAN

Boston

I have just returned from Boston.
It is the only thing to do if you find yourself up there.
FRED ALLEN

Clear out eight hundred thousand people and preserve it as a museum piece.
FRANK LLOYD WRIGHT

If I lived there, I'd move.
SARAH VAUGHAN

When I go abroad I always sail from Boston because
it's such a pleasant place to get away from.
OLIVER HEREFORD

And this is good old Boston
The home of the beans and the cod
Where the Lowells talk to the Cabots
And the Cabots talk only to God.
JOHN COLLINS BOSSIDY

New York–born socialite Isabella Stewart, who married Mr. Jack Gardner of Boston, was never really accepted in Boston society, especially after she walked a lion cub down Tremont Street. When she was asked by a dowager to contribute to the Boston Charitable Eye and Ear Association, Mrs. Gardner replied, "I didn't know there was a charitable eye or ear in Boston."

Branson, Missouri

Vegas for people with no teeth.
DENNIS MILLER

Brazil

Brazil has money that inflates like a dead dog in the sun.
CLIVE JAMES

Brno

Thre are mny twns in Czechoslovakia wthout vwels,
but Brno is the lrgest one of thm all.
ART BUCHWALD

The Bronx

The Bronx?
No thonx.
OGDEN NASH

Calcutta

Calcutta contains about 6.7 of the ugliest people you ever saw in your life per square foot, every last one of them pissing in, shitting in, throwing their garbage in, washing in and drinking from the same tepid creek. They paste raisins to their heads to honor a deity who hasn't answered a single prayer in five thousand years but who has more arms than their military; they wear their sheets on their heads and sleep in the mud; and you can hear their ribs rattle as they bow down in homage to a robust cow who's strip-grazed their gardens of everything except curry.
P. J. O'ROURKE

I arrived in Calcutta and checked into a motel so posh it had a toxicologist on staff to make sure that the food and beverages did not kill the guests.

TELLER

I shall always be glad to have seen it—for the same reason Papa gave for being glad to have seen Lisbon—namely, "that it will be unnecessary ever to see it again."

WINSTON CHURCHILL

California

I've never been out of this country but I've been to California. Does that count?

BOB BERGLAND

California is a place in which a boom mentality and a sense of Chekhovian loss meet in uneasy suspension.

JOAN DIDION

I wouldn't live in California. All that sun makes you sterile.

ALAN ALDA

[Suggested motto:] The Screwy State.

ROBERT GRAVES

California audiences applaud whenever a musician hesitates long enough to turn a page.

LEONARD MICHAELS

It is the land of perpetual pubescence, where cultural lag is mistaken for renaissance.

ASHLEY MONTAGU

Living in California adds ten years to a man's life.
And those extra ten years I'd like to spend in New York.

HARRY RUBY

Most people in California come from somewhere else. They moved to California so they could name their kids Rainbow or Mailbox, and purchase tubular Swedish furniture without getting laughed at. It's a tenet also in California that the fiber of your clothing is equivalent to your moral fiber. Your "lifestyle" (as they say) is your ethic. This means that in California you don't really have to do anything, except look healthy, think good thoughts and pat yourself on the back about what a good person you are. And waiters in California want to be called by their first name. I don't know why.

IAN SHOALES

California reminds me of the popular American Protestant concept of Heaven: There is always a reasonable flow of new arrivals; one meets many—not all— of one's friends; people spend a good deal of their time congratulating one another about the fact that they are there; discontent would be unthinkable; and the newcomer is slightly disconcerted to realize that now, the devil having been banished and virtue being triumphant, nothing terribly interesting can ever happen again.

GEORGE F. KENNAN

Canada

Canada is the vichyssoise of nations: Cold, half-French, and difficult to stir.
STUART KEATE

The symbol of contemporary Canada is the beaver, that industrious rodent
whose destiny it was to furnish hats that warmed better brains than his own.
ROY DANIELLS

A few acres of snow.
VOLTAIRE

Canada is a country whose main exports are hockey players and cold fronts.
Our main imports are baseball players and acid rain.
PIERRE TRUDEAU

Canada is a country so square that even the
female impersonators are women.
RICHARD BRENNER

Canada is the only country in the world that knows
how to live without an identity.
MARSHALL MCLUHAN

When I was there I found their jokes like their roads—very long
and not very good, leading to a little tin point of a spire which has been
remorselessly obvious for miles without seeming to get any nearer.
SAMUEL BUTLER

America's attic.
PATRICK ANDERSON

Americans know as much about Canada as straight people know about gays.
SCOTT THOMPSON

Cancún

Cancún was planned as a utopian city of parks, low-rise hotels,
and high-end tourists. But after the peso crashed in 1982, Mexicans
desperate for foreign exchange relaxed the restrictions on Cancún. Hotel
towers rose cheek by jowl; shopping malls sprouted; sewage flooded the
lagoon, and drug money flowed into the economy. Cheap package deals
brought in the rowdy spring-break crowd.
JONATHAN TOURTELLOT

Chattanooga

Missionary Ridge overlooks Chattanooga, and few will envy it.
WILLIAM MANCHESTER

Chicago

This vicious, stinking zoo, this mean-grinning, mace-smelling
boneyard of a city: an elegant rockpile of a monument to everything cruel
and stupid and corrupt in the human spirit.
HUNTER S. THOMPSON

Chicago has a strange metaphysical elegance of death about it.
CLAES OLDENBURG

Most cities have a smell of their own. Chicago smells like it's not sure.
ALAN KING

Chicago has only two seasons: winter and the Fourth of July.
LEWIS GRIZZARD

Chicago is not the most corrupt American city—
it's the most theatrically corrupt.
STUDS TERKEL

Here is the difference between Dante, Milton and me.
They wrote about hell and never saw the place. I wrote about Chicago
after looking the town over for years and years.
CARL SANDBURG

In Chicago, it is unwise to take your eyes off any asset
smaller than a locomotive.
KEITH WHEELER

A façade of skyscrapers facing a lake and behind the façade
every type of dubiousness.
E. M. FORSTER

China

I wouldn't mind seeing China if I could come back the same day.
PHILIP LARKIN

The bricklaying of contemporary China would shame a backyard amateur in Arkansas. The architecture is ghastly. In the newest and grandest buildings cement is cracked, taps don't work, escalators are out of order. Respect hygiene, proclaim the street posters, but the public lavatories are vile. . . . Though it is true that the Chinese-made elevators in my Shanghai hotel were the politest I have ever used, with buttons marked Please Open and Please Close, still I felt that all the courtesy in the world would not much avail us if we ever got stuck halfway.

JAN MORRIS

Very big, China.
NOËL COWARD

Cleveland

The mistake by the lake.
ANONYMOUS

Colombo, Sri Lanka

By midday in Colombo, the heat is so unbearable that the streets are empty save for thousands of Englishmen taking mad dogs for walks.
SPIKE MILLIGAN

Coney Island

On a visit to New York, the Russian novelist Maxim Gorky was taken to Coney Island. After a full day in the crowded amusement park, he was asked by his host what he thought of it. "What a sad people you must be!" Gorky replied.

Connecticut

Little Connecticut, with but 4,800 square miles of area,
lies just outside New York City, and is made up, in almost equal parts,
of golf links and squalid factory towns. There is a university called Yale at
New Haven. The people of Connecticut, in the early days, were very sharp
traders—in fact, swindlers. They made nutmegs of wood, and sold them
in New York. The nickname, Nutmeg State, clings to this day.

H. L. MENCKEN

Cyprus

Realizing that they will never be a world power,
the Cypriots have decided to be a world nuisance.

GEORGE MIKES

Dallas

To define Dallas is to add a whole new humongous dimension to bad.

MOLLY IVINS

Dallas is a city that honors the man who can buy a piece of art
more than the artist who creates one.

A. C. GREENE

Dallas reminds me of Hungary.

KARL LAGERFELD

Damascus

In Damascus, avoid eating in outdoor cafes around 8 P.M. That's when the
street sweepers make their rounds spraying pesticide.

CAILIN BOYLE

Darien

I once went to Darien . . . and a woman took me through
the neighborhood, describing all the houses and how much they'd cost.
My niece was with me and didn't seem surprised. Later I asked, "Why did she
talk about money so much?" And my niece said, "I think she was pleased to
be living in a district where no harm could come to her."

QUENTIN CRISP

Delaware

This is a small and measly state, owned by a single family,
the Du Ponts. They made their money manufacturing explosives.
Now they spend it quarreling among themselves. Most of Delaware is but two
or three feet above sea level. It has no large city, and no person of
any consequence has lived in it for half a century.

H. L. MENCKEN

A state that has three counties when the tide is out, and two when it is in.

JOHN JAMES INGALLS

Delhi

Delhi is the capital of the losing streak. It is the metropolis of the crossed
wire, the missed appointment, the puncture, the wrong number.

JAN MORRIS

Denmark

Denmark is no vacation paradise. It is cold and rainy and dark except for June and July, when it's extremely expensive.

GARRISON KEILLOR

Denver

Denver was not premeditated—it just happened.

ALICE POLK

Is everyone who lives in Denver automatically a member of the Mile High Club?

AARON SUGARMAN

Des Moines

Outside town there is a big sign that says:
Welcome to Des Moines. This is what death is like.

BILL BRYSON

Detroit

Cleveland without the glitter.

ANONYMOUS

England

England, the heart of a rabbit in the body of a lion, the jaws of a serpent in an abode of popinjays.

EUSTACHE DESCHAMPS

The Romans invaded England in 54 B.C. and discovered what every tourist
has discovered since: England is an aquarium, not a nation.
RITA MAE BROWN

England's a place where it's much more difficult to
buy something than to *sell* something.
STANLEY KUBRICK

So little, England. Little music. Little art. Timid. Tasteful. Nice.
ALAN BENNETT

The only country in the world where being "too clever by half" is an insult.
A. A. GILL

There'll always be an England, even if it's in Hollywood.
BOB HOPE

The Equator

In every book I ever read
Of travels on the Equator
A plague, mysterious and dread,
Imperils the narrator.
HILAIRE BELLOC

Europe

Everything in Europe is lukewarm except the radiators. You could use the
radiators to make party ice. But nobody does. I'll bet you could walk from the
Ural Mountains to the beach at Biarritz and not find one rock-hard, crystal-
clear, fist-sized American ice cube. Ask for whiskey on the rocks, and you get
a single gray, crumbling leftover from some Lilliputian puddle freeze plopped

in a thimble of Scotch (for which you're charged like sin). And the phones don't work. They go "blat-blat" and "neek-neek" and "ugu-ugu-ugu." No two dial tones are alike. The busy signal sounds as if the phone is ringing. And when the phone rings you think the dog farted.

P. J. O'ROURKE

In England, everything is permitted unless it's forbidden.
In Germany, everything is forbidden unless it's permitted.
In Italy, everything is permitted even if it's forbidden.

ANONYMOUS

Fez, Morocco

The package tourists who sweep in and out of towns like Fez are a fortunate breed. Sealed off by their air-conditioned coaches from the dusty anarchy through which they move, protected from its assaults and treacheries by their well-trained handlers, they are immune from reality. They come, they take their photographs, they go away. It is a splendid way to travel. I returned from Fez to Tangier, exhausted, after four days. During that time, I had been harried by cheating merchants, felled by a bad stomach and threatened with grievous bodily harm by my guide because I refused to allow his rapacity. The congested alleys and lanes of the medina had quickly lost their charm. I recoiled from the ceaseless counterpoint of language in the marketplace and the clamorous enveloping crowds. I brought back with me on the long train ride not the redolence of spices but the stench of animal droppings, of heaps of rotting vegetables, of dripping, uncured hides destined for the tanneries. The cloying sourness of the medina seemed to cling to my clothes, to exude from the pores of my skin. Mostly, though, as the train crawled through sun-lit, semi-arid dereliction, there hovered before me the feral cunning that had darkened the face of my guide as he sought to terrorize me. It had been a pitiless performance. I thought I would rest for a day or two in Tangier before setting out in search of further adventure.

SHIVA NAIPAUL

Florence

I used to dislike Florence, its inadequate river, its medieval bankers' machicolated fortresses miscalled palaces, its inadequately Mediterranean climate and rainy rentier reminders of Bath and Cheltenham.

CYRIL CONNOLLY

Florida

In none of the forty-eight states does life leap so suddenly, in an hour's motor drive, from the suburban snooze to the primeval ooze.

ALISTAIR COOKE

Florida was the only wilderness in the world that attracted middle-aged pioneers.

JOHN McPHEE

My parents didn't want to move to Florida, but they
turned sixty, and that's the law.
JERRY SEINFELD

The land of phlegm.
STUEY STONE

Fort Worth

In Fort Worth, if a man carries an umbrella his manhood is suspect.
MARK RUSSELL

France

A relatively small and eternally quarrelsome country in
Western Europe, fountainhead of rationalist political manias, militarily
impotent, historically inglorious during the past century, democratically
bankrupt, Communist-infiltrated from top to bottom.
WILLIAM F. BUCKLEY, JR.

France is a nation devoted to the false hypothesis on which
it then builds marvelously logical structures.
GORE VIDAL

France is the most civilized country in the world and
doesn't care who knows it.
JOHN GUNTHER

France is a dog-hole.
WILLIAM SHAKESPEARE

France has neither winter nor summer nor morals—
apart from these drawbacks it is a fine country.

MARK TWAIN

How can anyone govern a nation that has 240 different kinds of cheese?

CHARLES DE GAULLE

We always have been, we are and I hope that we
always shall be detested in France.

DUKE OF WELLINGTON

In fine art, France is a nation of born pedants.

GEORGE BERNARD SHAW

Everything is on such a clear financial basis in France.
It is the simplest country to live in. No one makes things complicated
by becoming your friend for any obscure reason. If you want people to
like you, you have only to spend a little money.

ERNEST HEMINGWAY

France is the only country where the money falls apart
and you can't tear the toilet paper.

BILLY WILDER

Dogs smoke in France.

OZZY OSBOURNE

In America, only the successful writer is important, in France all writers are important, in England no writer is important, and in Australia you have to explain what a writer is.

GEOFFREY COTTRELL

Frankfurt

Frankfurt is a large, unfriendly financial center filled with dirty, gray office high-rises, thus earning it the title "the most Americanized city in Europe."

CHRIS HARRIS

Greece

Everything in Greece takes twice as long as it would anywhere else. In this country they just do not use time at all.

EVELYN WAUGH

Green Bay

In Green Bay, Wisconsin, ten bowling shirts are considered a great wardrobe.

GREG KOCH

Hawaii

It is not surprising that Hawaii is so popular. At a time when theme parks are all the rage, Hawaii is the biggest theme park in the world.

FRANK DEFORD

Holland

What wounds one's feeling in Holland is the perpetual consciousness
that the country has no business being there at all. You see it all below the
level of the water, soppy, hideous and artificial.

MATTHEW ARNOLD

Apart from cheese and tulips, the main product of the country is
advocaat, a drink made from lawyers.

ALAN COREN

Hollywood

Hollywood is like being nowhere and talking to nobody about nothing.

MICHELANGELO ANTONIONI

The complete reductio ad absurdum of civilization.

H. L. MENCKEN

People wear resort clothes, but actually Hollywood is an enormous factory.

MARIE-FRANCE PISIER

Hollywood is a place where people from Iowa mistake
each other for movie stars.

FRED ALLEN

Vomit, California.
MONTGOMERY CLIFT

Honolulu

Honolulu—it's got everything: Sand for the children,
sun for the wife, sharks for the wife's mother.
KED DODD

Houston

The city has been an act of real estate rather than an act of God or man.
ADA LOUISE HUXTABLE

The air was warm and rich and suggestive of fossil fuel.
JOAN DIDION

Houston is Los Angeles with the climate of Calcutta.
MOLLY IVINS

India

India: What mysteries does the very mention of the name not bring to mind?
(Answer: Mysteries of the Deep, Mysteries of the Arctic Wastes, the Lizzie
Borden Mystery, and Sweet Mystery of Life.)
ROBERT BENCHLEY

India is a geographical term. It is no more a united nation than the Equator.
WINSTON CHURCHILL

"Sub-" is no idle prefix in its application to this continent.
P. J. O'ROURKE

From the moment you set foot in India, you realize there's something different, something special in the air. Some say it's spiritual, others say it's cultural. I think it's a wicked combination of curry, cow shit, and breathtaking body odor; India has 900 million people, 200 million cows, and enough curry to turn the Pacific Ocean into a giant seafood stir-fry.
DOUG LANSKY

Indonesia

Virtually everything we were told in Indonesia turned out not to be true, sometimes almost immediately. The only exception to this was when [we] were told that something would happen immediately, in which case it turned out not to be true over an extended period of time.
DOUGLAS ADAMS

Iran

Persia consists of two parts: A desert with salt, and a desert without salt.
OLD SAYING

Ireland

Ireland has the honor of being the only country which never persecuted the Jews—because she never let them in.
JAMES JOYCE

The English should give Ireland home rule—
and reserve the motion picture rights.

WILL ROGERS

The trouble with Ireland is that it's a country full of genius,
but with absolutely no talent.

HUGH LEONARD

Italy, at least, has two things to balance its miserable
poverty and mismanagement: a lively intellectual movement and a good
climate. Ireland is Italy without these two.

JAMES JOYCE

Istanbul

In Istanbul, everything is named after Kemal Atatürk. (Atta boy, Atatürk!)

JOHN KRICH

Istanbul is difficult, of course, by its very nature. Atatürk's attempts to wish
logic and modernity upon it have failed, and it is as obscurantist, as devious
and as stubborn today as ever it was in the days of the Sultans. It is clogged
by the accumulated filth of the centuries, layered generation by generation
upon the original defecations of Byzantium. It is entramelled equally by age
and change, unravellable labyrinths of bazaars, desolate abortions of progres-
sive planning. The Golden Horn stirs but sluggishly, viscous with oil and
ordure: ever and ever again the city staggers into immobility, jammed by
some unseen and never-to-be-explained calamity round the corner.

JAN MORRIS

Italy

Italy is boot-shaped, for reasons lost in the mists of geology. The South is essentially agricultural, and administered by local land authorities, called the Mafia; the North is industrial, and run by tightly interlocked corporations, called the Mafia. The largest Italian city is New York, and is linked to the mainland by a highly specialized and efficient communications system, called the Mafia.

ALAN COREN

Anarchy tempered by bureaucracy.

GEORGE F. WILL

The smog, or whatever they call it, is terrible. There is no Italian word for smog, on the theory that, if you don't name it, it doesn't exist.

HERB CAEN

Japan

It's so far away . . . and then you have to eat all that raw fish, drink tepid rice wine and live in cardboard houses.

W. H. AUDEN

Jerusalem

My sympathies were tending towards the Arabs, but I was pushed to a more neutral position at four in the morning when I was awakened by the sound of moaning over a distorted loudspeaker. The American Colony Hotel is next door to a mosque. Every few hours mosques must broadcast renditions in Arabic of the phrases "Allah is Great, there is no God but Allah, and Mohammed is His Prophet." After 40 repetitions at 4 A.M. I could see why nerves are frayed in Jerusalem.

DAVID DALE

Kansas

Kansas is a state of the Union, but it is also a state of mind, a neurotic condition, a psychological phase, a symptom, indeed, something undreamed of in your philosophy, an inferiority complex against the tricks and manners of plutocracy—social, political and economic.

WILLIAM ALLEN WHITE

Historians have now definitely established that Juan Cabrillo, discoverer of California, was not looking for Kansas, thus setting a precedent that continues to this day.

WAYNE SHANNON

Key West

Key West got me down more than all the others. Maybe it was expectations. The literary haunt of Hemingway, vacation hideaway of President Harry Truman, an end-of-the-road town celebrated in the songs of Jimmy Buffett. What I found instead was a packed-to-the-lightposts tourist-tacky town full of chain restaurants and a handsome Victorian mansion converted into the local Hooters. Free enterprise has been allowed to run amok, with anything resembling a real retailer driven out in favor of an endless string of T-shirt stores, time-share sellers, and curio shops.

GARY A. WARNER

La Jolla

Nothing but a climate and a lot of meaningless chi-chi.

RAYMOND CHANDLER

Lake Erie

[Suggested Motto:] Contains Some Actual Water.

DAVE BARRY

Las Vegas

Las Vegas is Everyman's cut-rate Babylon. Not far away there is,
or was, a roadside lunch counter and over it a sign proclaiming in three
words that a Roman emperor's orgy is now a democratic institution . . .
"Topless Pizza Lunch."

ALISTAIR COOKE

A natural habitat, where the unnatural runs rampant.

ROBIN FINN

Smack-dab in the middle of the desert, surrounded by hideous mountains
that look like slag heaps, Las Vegas has no river, no lake, no forest, no penin-
sula, no promontory, no buttes, not even a dale or a rivulet to recommend it
topographically. Brutally hot in the summer, despite the locals' addled ration-
alizations that "it's a dry heat, so you don't feel it that much," Las Vegas is a

masterpiece of cultural *trompe l'oeil,* a vast municipal gauntlet that the United States of America has thrown down to the rest of the world.

The challenge to the world runs something like this:

"This city was built on a whim by gangsters in the 1940s. There aren't any natural wonders here. The only interesting building is a glass replica of the Great Pyramids right across the street from a $39-a-night motel. The only thing you can do in this town is lose your life's savings and then go listen to Wayne Newton sing *Danke Schöen.* Of course, we will throw in a complimentary buffet."

JOE QUEENAN

The most insidious influence of Las Vegas is its destruction of wonder: The wonder of sex, the wonder of chance, and the wonder of oneself. Everything is settled fast in Las Vegas. Like the lava outcroppings of its desert, Nevada has become a molten overflow of the American passion for excess. It is a long way from Plymouth Rock.

NEIL MORGAN

It is highwayman and whore on the desert road, a city
both veneer and venereal, dedicated to waste and excess,
heartless and without a heart; a town where, probably, nothing
good or worthwhile has ever happened, nor ever will.

TREVOR FISHLOCK

Las Vegas was never meant to be seen by day.

PETER S. BEAGLE

Latvia

Latvia is not a good place in which to get sick or require hospitalization.

INARA ASTRIDA PUNGA AND WILLIAM HOUGH

Liverpool

This god-forsaken city, with a climate so evil that no self-respecting singer would ever set foot in it! It is a catarrhal place that has been the cause through the centuries of the nasal Liverpool accent.

SIR THOMAS BEECHAM

London

London is too full of fogs—and serious people. Whether the fogs produce the serious people or whether the serious people produce the fogs, I don't know, but the whole thing rather gets on my nerves.

OSCAR WILDE

London, that great cesspool into which all the loungers of the Empire are irresistibly drained.

SIR ARTHUR CONAN DOYLE

A place you go to get bronchitis.

FRAN LEBOWITZ

London, like a bowl of viscid human fluid, boils sullenly over the rim of its encircling hills and slops messily and uglily into the home counties.

H. G. WELLS

A foggy, dead-alive city like a dying ant-heap. London was created for rich young men to shop in, dine in, ride in, get married in,

go to theatres in, and die in as respected householders.
It is a city for the unmarried upper class, not for the poor.
CYRIL CONNOLLY

Crowds without company, and dissipation without pleasure.
EDWARD GIBBON

I'm leaving because the weather is too good.
I hate London when it's not raining.
GROUCHO MARX

Our primary cultural activity in London was changing money. We had to do this a lot because the dollar is very weak. Europeans use the dollar primarily to apply shoe polish. So every day we'd go to one of the money-changing places that are all over London, and we'd exchange some dollars for British money, which consists of the "pound" and a wide variety of mutant coins whose sizes and shapes are unrelated to their values, and then we'd look for something to eat that had been invented in this century, such as pizza, and we'd buy three slices for what we later realized was $247.50, and then we'd change some money again. Meanwhile, the Japanese tourists were exchanging *their* money for items such as Westminster Abbey.
DAVE BARRY

I'm afraid I always feel London is very unhealthy—I can hear fat Caribbean germs pattering after me in the Underground.
PHILIP LARKIN

The monstrous tuberosity of civilized life, the capital of England.
THOMAS CARLYLE

When it's three o'clock in New York, it's still 1938 in London.
BETTE MIDLER

In London they don't like you if you're still alive.
HARVEY FIERSTEIN

Los Angeles

It's a jolly greedy city. It's a city devoted to pleasure, self-indulgence,
prettiness, health, immortality and gracefulness. People are devoting so
much time to avoiding death they haven't got much time for leading their life.
JONATHAN MILLER

[In Los Angeles] the car is the extension of the self and
the self is measured by abdominal tautness.
DAVID J. JEFFERSON

Living in L.A. is like not having a date on Saturday night.
CANDICE BERGEN

L.A. to me is like Vegas—but the losers stay in town.
JERRY SEINFELD

The light blue haze in the lower canyon was like a thin smoke
from slowly burning money. Even the sea looked precious through it. . . .
I had never seen the Pacific look so small.
ROSS MACDONALD

If you ever tilted the map of the U.S.A. very sharply, Los Angeles
is the spot where everything would spill out.
FRANK LLOYD WRIGHT

The chief products of Los Angeles are novelizations, salad,
game-show hosts, points, muscle tone, mini-series and rewrites.

They export all of these items with the twin exceptions of muscle tone and points, neither of which seem to travel well.

FRAN LEBOWITZ

It's a great place to live, but I wouldn't want to visit there.

MARK TWAIN

Louisiana

They say Louisiana is somewhat like a banana republic, say Guatemala. That's not true. They speak better English in Guatemala.

JACK KNEECE

Luxembourg

On a clear day, from the terrace of the Salon de Philatelie, you can't see Luxembourg at all. This is because a tree is in the way.

ALAN COREN

Maine

As Maine goes, so goes Vermont.

JAMES A. FARLEY

There are only two things that ever make the front page in Maine papers. One is a forest fire and the other is when a New Yorker shoots a moose instead of the game warden.

GROUCHO MARX

Malibu

Malibu tends to astonish and disappoint those who have never before seen it, and yet its very name remains, in the imagination of people all over the world, a kind of shorthand for the easy life. I had not before 1971 and will probably not again live in a place with a Chevrolet named after it.

JOAN DIDION

Manchester

I would like to live in Manchester, England. The transition between Manchester and death would be unnoticeable.

MARK TWAIN

The Mediterranean

Torquay with extra sun.

SIMON JENKINS

Melbourne

I couldn't imagine a better place for making a film on the end of the world.

AVA GARDNER

Mexico

Poor Mexico, so far from God and so near to the United States!

PORFIRIO DÍAZ

Miami

We had elected to move voluntarily to Miami. We wanted our child to benefit from the experience of growing up in a community that is constantly being enriched by a diverse and ever-changing infusion of tropical diseases. Also they have roaches down there you could play polo with.

DAVE BARRY

Miami: Mecca for the retired refugee; God's waiting room.

JOHN LEGUIZAMO

It's a challenge for most Americans to visit Miami because it's bilingual. I still don't know what the other language is besides Spanish.

DAVE BARRY

Miami Beach

Where neon goes to die.

LENNY BRUCE

The Midwest

An Eliot landscape where the spiritual air is "thoroughly small and dry." If I stay here any longer I shall either take to mysticism . . . or buy a library of pornographic books.

W. H. AUDEN

I doubt if there is anything in the world uglier than a Midwestern city.

FRANK LLOYD WRIGHT

Bland, boring and beige.

DAN S. KAERCHER

Minneapolis and St. Paul

[They] are nicknamed the Twin Cities. They are divided by
the Mississippi River, and united by the belief that the inhabitants
of the other side of the river are inferior.

TREVOR FISHLOCK

Minnesota

[Suggested motto:] Home of the Late April Slush.

CALVIN TRILLIN

The state seal shows a farmer, a waterfall, a forest, and an Indian riding
into the sunset. It should be changed to ice cubes rampant on a field of white,
a grinning barefoot Swede in a Grain Belt Beer T-shirt riding a snowmobile,
and a shivering visitor whose stricken breath is freezing into ice crystals.

CHARLES KURALT

Mississippi

When you're in Mississippi, the rest of America doesn't seem real.
And when you're in the rest of America, Mississippi doesn't seem real.

BOB PARRIS MOSES

Montana

A large cow-intensive state located near Canada.

DAVE BARRY

In Montana, Velveeta cheese is in the gourmet section of the supermarket.

STUEY STONE

Monte Carlo

The whole town had an air of being Parisian, but not Parisian enough.

ARNOLD BENNETT

Monterey, California

They fish for tourists now, not pilchards, and that species
they are not likely to wipe out.

JOHN STEINBECK

Myrtle Beach, South Carolina

Myrtle Beach is the sociological equivalent of the inside of a single man's refrigerator. Driving to the [golf] course from our motel, I got an inkling of what the world would be like if wives did not exist. There were gas stations, cheap motels, a topless karaoke bar, liquor stores, pawn shops, hangar-sized fried-food restaurants, golf-equipment stores that stayed open until ten, and very little else. A white frame bungalow that looked like a farmer's vegetable stand turned out to be a used-golf-ball store. You can find anything you want in Myrtle Beach, as long as it isn't broccoli or a diaper.

DAVID OWEN

Naples, Florida

Sunlit hell.

EDMUND WILSON

Naples, Italy

"See Naples and die." Well, I do not know that one would necessarily die after merely seeing it, but to attempt to live there might turn out a little differently.

MARK TWAIN

Nebraska

Nebraska is proof that Hell is full, and the dead walk the earth.

LIZ WINSTON

New England

The most serious charge which can be brought against New England is not Puritanism but February.

JOSEPH WOOD KRUTCH

There's something overdone and stagy about a New England spring.

LEWIS LAPHAM

I wonder if anybody ever reached the age of thirty-five in New England without wanting to kill himself.

BARRETT WENDELL

New Hampshire

I live in New Hampshire so I can get a better view of Vermont.

MAXFIELD PARRISH

New Jersey

New Jersey looks like the back of an old radio.
JOSH GREENFELD

New Jersey announced today that they were adopting a new license-plate slogan: "Try Our Creamy Thick Shakes."
DAVID LETTERMAN

A state where political honesty is usually discussed during a prosecutor's summation.
JIMMY BRESLIN

The Holland Tunnel was built so commuters can go to New Jersey without being seen.
FRED ALLEN

New Jersey's a fabulous place to leave.
SUSAN SARANDON

New Orleans

Everyone complains about how bad New Orleans drivers are. In a strict sense, no doubt, it's true. Everybody's drunk or driving that way. In fact, the law requires new drivers in Louisiana to pass the test drunk. It's the only way to survive. New cars sold here all come equipped with air bags and two sizes of drink holders, a large one for beer and a smaller one for bourbon. Drive-by daiquiri places are placed at the entrance of shopping-mall parking lots. Shoppers drop three bucks in the machine and get four ounces of sweetened alcohol to help them shop. Consequently, driving here is a nightmare for orderly people from the rest of America. There are hundreds of casualties when snowbirds from the East come through here in the winter on their way to the Gulf.
ANDREI CODRESCU

New York

A third-rate Babylon.
H. L. MENCKEN

Skyscraper National Park.
KURT VONNEGUT

On any person who desires such queer prizes, New York will bestow
the gift of loneliness and the gift of privacy.
E. B. WHITE

If a day goes by and I haven't been slain, I'm happy.
CAROL LEIFER

A marriage, to be happy, needs an exterior threat.
New York provides that threat.
GARRISON KEILLOR

I had to move to New York for health reasons. I'm very paranoid
and New York is the only place where my fears are justified.
ANITA WISE

Some people say Paris is more esthetic than New York. Well,
in New York you don't have time to have an esthetic because it takes
half the day to go downtown and half the day to go uptown.
ANDY WARHOL

The nation's thyroid gland.
CHRISTOPHER MORLEY

I love New York. I've got a gun.

CHARLES BARKLEY

No other city in the United States can divest the visitor of so
much money with so little enthusiasm. In Dallas, they take away with gusto;
in New Orleans, with a bow; in San Francisco, with a wink and a grin.
In New York, you're lucky if you get a grunt.

FLETCHER KNEBEL

New York is the only city in the world where you can get deliberately
run down on the sidewalk by a pedestrian.

RUSSELL BAKER

On a New York subway you get fined for spitting,
but you can throw up for nothing.

LEWIS GRIZZARD

When you leave New York, you are astonished at how clean
the rest of the world is. Clean is not enough.

FRAN LEBOWITZ

New Zealand

Terrible Tragedy of the South Seas. Three million people trapped alive!

TOM SCOTT

A Maori fisherman, the legends say,
Dredged up New Zealand in a single day.
I've seen the catch, and here's my parting crack—
It's undersized; for God's sake throw it back!

WYNFORD VAUGHAN-THOMAS

A little piece of Victoriana in the Antipodes.
TONY SIMPSON

Before sailing from London, five people told me that you can always tell a Wellington man because he holds onto his hat when he walks round the corner of a street because the wind blows round the corners. Everybody in the ship coming out to whom I mentioned New Zealand told me the story again, until at last I thought of having a small placard hanging round my neck with "I know how to tell a Wellington man," or "Please don't tell me the story of the Wellington man and the wind; I know it."
MAURICE BARING

When I was there it seemed to be shut.
CLEMENT FREUD

Nome, Alaska

If you don't believe hell freezes over, you haven't been to Nome.
LUCKY SEVERSON

Normal, Illinois

The town of Normal itself is, at first glance, very solid. Main Street has a stationery store, a used furniture store, a new furniture store, a lingerie shop, and several bars. We were directed to a place called the Posh Nosh for lunch. I ordered gumbo. This being the Midwest, gumbo was turkey rice soup with a sliced hot dog in it.

ANDREI CODRESCU

North Dakota

In South Dakota we used to say that the only good thing that comes out of North Dakota is Highway 81.

TOM BROKAW

The North Sea

The same old thing. A gray-green expanse of smudgy waters grinning angrily at one with white foam-ridges, and over all a cheerless, unglowing canopy, apparently made of wet blotting paper. . . . It isn't for nothing that the North Sea is also called the German Ocean.

JOSEPH CONRAD

Northern Europe

I do not find Northern Europe an ideal zone for human habitation. It is a fine place for industrial productivity, but its climate breeds puritans and the terrible dictates of the Protestant Work Ethic. The Romans were right to pull out when they did.

KENNETH TYNAN

Oakland

When you get there, there isn't any there there.
GERTRUDE STEIN

The trouble with Oakland is that when you get there, it's there.
HERB CAEN

Oklahoma

In 1889 the U.S. government opened up the Oklahoma territory, which resulted in the famous "Oklahoma land rush" as thousands of would-be settlers came racing in to look around, resulting in the famous "rush to get the hell back out of Oklahoma."
DAVE BARRY

It was fascinating to be in a place where the word "cholesterol" never crosses anyone's lips, despite a local predilection for eating a piece of beef at least once every three hours. One day we had beef sausage at breakfast, burgers for lunch and beef ribs for dinner. Here is a state where either you're driving around looking at cows—or eating them.
DEBORAH SOLOMON

Oregon

Always get the skin rash up here. And athlete's foot all the way to the ankle. The moisture. It's certainly no wonder that this area has two or three natives a month take that one-way dip—it's either drown your blasted self or rot.
KEN KESEY

Ottawa

A sub-arctic lumber village converted by royal mandate
into a political cockpit.

GOLDWIN SMITH

Palm Beach

A lot of elderly rich women seeing how small they can get their dogs.

RITA RUDNER

Panama

It's not like they make or grow anything. The whole country is based on
international banking and a canal the United States can take back any time
it wants with one troop of Boy Scouts.

P. J. O'ROURKE

Paris

One thinks of Paris as a woman, rather pretty, somewhat
regardless of morals and decidedly slovenly of person; craving admiration,
but too indolent to earn it by keeping herself presentable; covering up the
dirt on a piquant face with rice powder; wearing paste jewels in her earlobes
in an effort to distract criticism from the fact that the ears themselves
stand in need of soap and water.

IRVIN S. COBB

I've been to Paris France and I've been to Paris Paramount.
Paris Paramount is better.

ERNST LUBITSCH

An heir to millions, native of Cincinnati, was dining alone in Paris when he thought he detected a "come hither" look in [the] eyes of the prettiest girl he had ever seen. "She jumped into a cab," he told his friends when he returned to America, "and I jumped into another. 'Follow that girl,' I commanded. Down the Champs Elysées we raced, across the Seine, and up the Boulevard Raspail. When she alighted at a studio building in the heart of the Left Bank, I was only a few steps behind her. I caught her on the landing of her apartment, and with a happy sigh I will never forget, she melted into my arms." "What happened after that?" his friends asked breathlessly. The excitement died down in the heir's voice. "After that," he admitted, "it was just like Cincinnati."

BENNETT CERF

Did you know . . . that the sun doesn't shine from November to March in Paris? The City of Lights' best-kept secret is that, for its many charms, it still has basically the same weather as London. Or Cleveland. Among my amusements is listening to folks back from Paris, saying it was great except they had bad luck with the weather. It's not luck.

RICHARD REEVES

Philadelphia

We stayed in Philadelphia for five weeks, and gradually came to feel almost at home there—that is, if anybody not born in the town can ever feel at home in Philadelphia.

H. L. MENCKEN

Six months residence here would justify suicide.

HERBERT SPENCER

A metropolis sometimes known as the City of Brotherly Love but more accurately as the City of Bleak November Afternoons.

S. J. PERELMAN

They have Easter egg hunts in Philadelphia, and if the kids don't find the eggs, they get booed.

BOB UECKER

Phnom Penh

Phnom Penh is bad; out of Phnom Penh is worse. Other than to the ruins at Angkor, nobody goes out. There are the five—or is it ten?—million land mines. The vipers, the two kinds of cobras, the poisonous banded kraits. Also the bacteriological soup of Japanese encephalitis, typhoid, and malaria. Also the fact that the army and the police have not been paid in four months and are getting hungry. Also that the roads are positively African, but with all the land mines and snakes, the first rule of travel in Cambodia is never step off the road.

PATRICK SYMMES

Phoenix

An oasis of ugliness in the midst of a beautiful wasteland.

EDWARD ABBEY

Phuket

Phuket, it is generally agreed, is a tourist shithole—best served for anthropological studies of fat German men who wear Speedos.

ROLF POTTS

Pittsburgh

Abandon it.

FRANK LLOYD WRIGHT

Poland

Poland is now a totally independent nation, and it has managed
to greatly improve its lifestyle thanks to the introduction of modern
Western conveniences such as food.

DAVE BARRY

In the past few centuries, Poland has become known as "the airplane lavatory
of Europe"—dirty, subject to turbulence, and almost constantly occupied.

CHRIS HARRIS

Rome

Rome's just a city like anywhere else. A vastly overrated city, I'd say.
It trades on belief just as Stratford trades on Shakespeare.

ANTHONY BURGESS

Rome has more churches and less preaching in them than any city in the world.

WILL ROGERS

Rome reminds me of a man who lives by exhibiting to
travelers his grandmother's corpse.

JAMES JOYCE

Rome, Italy, is an example of what happens when the buildings
in a city last too long.

ANDY WARHOL

In Rome . . . at first, you are full of regrets that Michelangelo died, but by and by you only regret that you did not see him do it.

MARK TWAIN

The Rubicon

This river that makes so great a figure in history is nothing more than a muddy stream that we would hardly dignify with the name of a brook in America. I have been exceedingly disappointed in the classic streams of Italy that have been so often sung by the poets; I have found them generally yellow, dirty, and turbid.

WASHINGTON IRVING

Russia

Russia is the only country in the world you can be homesick for while you're still in it.

JOHN UPDIKE

I never think I'm going to get out of Russia. Something about the airport says, "We are closed for no reason all of a sudden. Try again . . . someday."

HENRY ROLLINS

San Francisco

San Francisco: Hollywood pretending to be New York.
JULES SIEGEL

The coldest winter I ever spent was a summer in San Francisco.
MARK TWAIN

Santa Fe

Impression of Santa Fe as having become largely a sucker town. Many Indians and Mexicans on the street. Ten Gallon hats everywhere. We went to dine at a Mexican restaurant run by two eastern college girls.
SHERWOOD ANDERSON

Santa Monica

The most characteristic Santa Monica effect, that air of dispirited abandon which suggests that the place survives only as illustration of a boom gone bankrupt, evidence of some irreversible flaw in the laissez-faire small-business ethic.
JOAN DIDION

Seattle

[Seattle is] surrounded by the soft, the gray, and the moist, as if it is being digested by an oyster.
TOM ROBBINS

Selma, Alabama

Just as in the anatomy of man, every nation must have its hind part.

ROBERT INDIANA

Singapore

Disneyland with the death penalty.

EVE JONES

The South

Storytelling and copulation are the two chief forms of amusement in the South. They're inexpensive and easy to procure.

ROBERT PENN WARREN

South Dakota

It is said that as a somewhat deflated George Armstrong Custer lay bleeding in the Montana dirt at the Little Big Horn, he turned his glazed and dimming eyes east and said, "At least we don't have to go back through South Dakota."

TIM CAHILL

Southern California

In a thousand years or so, when the first archaeologists from beyond the date-line unload their boat on the sands of Southern California, they will find much the same scene as confronted the Franciscan Missionaries. A dry landscape will extend from the ocean to the mountains. Bel Air and Beverly Hills will lie naked save for scrub and cactus, all their flimsy multitude of architectural styles turned long ago to dust, while the horned toad and the turkey buzzard leave their faint imprint on the dunes that will drift on Sunset Boulevard.

EVELYN WAUGH

There's nothing wrong with Southern California that a rise in the ocean level wouldn't cure.

ROSS MACDONALD

Spain

Spain imports tourists and exports chambermaids.

CARLOS FUENTES

Stratford Upon Avon

Anne Hathaway's cottage and Mary Arden's cottage are sufficiently beautiful, with their brilliant gardens, to soften the most obdurate foe of quaintness. But like all the other high spots in Stratford, they have been provided with postcard stands and with neat custodians whose easy, mechanical Poet-worship had me looking sharply to see if they were plugged into the wall. All of Stratford, in fact, suggests powdered history—add hot water and stir and you have a delicious, nourishing Shakespeare. The inhabitants of the town occupy themselves with painting SWEET ARE THE USES OF ADVERSITY around the rims of moustache cups for the tourist trade; the wide, cement-paved main is street fringed with literary hot dog stands; and in the narrow lanes adjoining, wrinkled little beldames of Tudor houses wearily serve out their time as tea rooms.

MARGARET HALSEY

Switzerland

Switzerland is simply a large, humpy, solid rock, with a thin skin of grass stretched over it.

MARK TWAIN

The only interesting thing that can happen in a Swiss bedroom is suffocation by feather mattress.

DALTON TRUMBO

In Italy, for 30 years under the Borgias, they had warfare, terror, murder, bloodshed, but they produced Michaelangelo, Leonardo da Vinci and the Renaissance. In Switzerland, they had brotherly love, five hundred years of democracy and peace—and what did they produce? The cuckoo clock.

ORSON WELLES, IN *The Third Man*

One quiet afternoon, I strolled around the village, marveling at the foaming river that rushes through its heart and the uncanny neatness of the buildings. In the heart of the town is the oldest structure—a peak-roofed wooden house inscribed 1632; it stands next to an almost identical building marked 1966 and looks every bit as sturdy and fresh. Here and there, three-man crews were sweeping the streets and gutters. I watched them for a while and it suddenly occurred to me that they were doing something that could only happen in Switzerland. They were cleaning up the clean.

HERB CAEN

The first time I passed through the country I had the impression it was swept down with a broom from one end to the other every morning by housewives who dumped all the dirt on Italy.

ERNESTO SABATO

Sydney

Manchester [England] with a harbor backdrop.
ROBERT MORLEY

Tel Aviv

Whatever Tel Aviv lacked, there was no shortage of cement block.
S. J. PERELMAN

Tempe, Arizona

Tempe—where a baby's first words are often, "But it's a *dry* heat."
DENNIS MILLER

Texas

The place where there are the most cows and the least milk
and the most rivers and the least water in them, and where you can
look the farthest and see the least.
H. L. MENCKEN

Like most passionate nations Texas has its own private history based on,
but not limited by, facts.
JOHN STEINBECK

The only thing that smells worse than an oil refinery is a feedlot.
Texas has a lot of both.
MOLLY IVINS

If I owned two plantations and one was located in Texas and the other one was in Hell, I would rent out the one in Texas and live on the other one.
PHILIP SHERIDAN

Thailand

Thailand is Disneyland. Go to any part of Thailand and they have *rides:* a ride on a raft, a ride on an elephant, a trip to a butterfly farm.
MARGO KAUFMAN

Tokyo

Tokyo . . . looks as if it were hit by an anti-charm missile. It had the bad fortune of being almost entirely rebuilt after World War II, during what architectural historians refer to as the Age of Making Everything Look Like a Municipal Parking Garage, but Without the Warmth.
DAVE BARRY

The Tropics

The four R's of tropical travel: rats, roaches, rain, and rip-off.
BARBARA ANN CURCIO

Turkey

Turkey is aptly named.
HOWARD OGDEN

Vatican City

I just came back from the Vatican. Very disillusioning.
They have a Hard Rock.
DENNIS MILLER

Venice, California

Where the debris meets the sea.
ANONYMOUS

Venice, Italy

It is possible to dislike Venice, and to entertain the sentiment in a responsible
and intelligent manner.
HENRY JAMES

Venice is like eating an entire box of chocolate liqueurs in one go.
TRUMAN CAPOTE

A Renaissance Disneyland with entrance fees only the rich can afford.
Private Eye

A city that must be seen to be disbelieved.
HENRY R. LUCE

Coney Island with pigeons.
IRENE KAMPEN

Wonderful city. Streets full of water. Please advise.
ROBERT BENCHLEY *(telegram)*

Wadi Halfa, Sudan

In Wadi Halfa, the hottest part of the day lasts from nine
in the morning until nine at night.

MICHAEL PALIN

Wales

The land of my fathers. My fathers can have it.

DYLAN THOMAS

There are still parts of Wales where the only concession
to gaiety is a striped shroud.

GWYN THOMAS

Washington, D.C.

Washington is the only place where sound travels faster than light.

C. V. R. THOMPSON

Washington is an endless series of mock palaces clearly built for clerks.

ADA LOUISE HUXTABLE

Washington is a city of Southern efficiency and Northern charm.

JOHN F. KENNEDY

West Virginia

Hey, I've been to West Virginia.
Be glad you live on this side of the culture warp.

DENNIS MILLER

Winnipeg

Winnipeg is like Fargo, North Dakota, without the action.
BILLY JAY

You can skip Winnipeg.
RUDOLF NUREYEV

The World

It is not a fragrant world.
RAYMOND CHANDLER

I have recently been around the world and have formed a poor opinion of it.
SIR THOMAS BEECHAM

We are told that when Jehovah created the world he saw
that it was good. What would he say now?
GEORGE BERNARD SHAW

I suggested that she take a trip around the world. "Oh, I know,"
returned the lady, yawning with ennui, "but there's so many other
places I want to see first."
S. J. PERELMAN

TRAVEL TIPS

(If You *Must* Go . . .)

Avoid all airplane travel except by privately owned jets operated for the benefit of America's twenty-five most indispensable CEOs.

RUSSELL BAKER

Whenever possible, avoid airlines which have anyone's first name in their titles, like Bob's International Airline or Air Fred.

MISS PIGGY

Never board a commercial aircraft if the pilot is wearing a tank top.

DAVE BARRY

Never play peek-a-boo with a child on a long plane trip.
There's no end to the game. Finally I grabbed him by the bib and said,
"Look, it's always gonna be me!"

RITA RUDNER

The airline industry makes the hierarchy of humans quite clear. On top are first-class patrons and members of Executive Premier and other elite groups. They are followed by business-class customers and on down to the peasants who fly coach.

As a corollary, it may be tempting for people who usually fly coach but who, for whatever reason, are flying business class to believe themselves inferior to the flight attendants in that cabin. This, of course, is utterly, completely and absolutely true. Every society must have rules. Don't fight it. However, business-class interlopers need not feel they must constantly seek the approval of business-class flight attendants. For instance, you need not accept food each time it is offered. And it is not necessary to ask the attendant if you can get her anything. Also, don't ask her if she recommends the cannelloni agl'ortaggi in salsa di peperoni dolci or the filet mignon. *It's airplane food!*

MATT RICHTEL

If you're going to America, bring your own food.

FRAN LEBOWITZ

Don't talk to the crazy people on the street, even though
they may seem fun to be with.

Citypack: New York

You have to run ahead of people sometimes and try to kill them.

MELISSA ZEGANS,
on how to catch a cab in Manhattan

Tip to out-of-town visitors: If you buy something here in New York and want to have it shipped home, be suspicious if the clerk tells you they don't need your name and address.

DAVID LETTERMAN

To younger [American] travelers: Don't embarrass us all by wearing a "Gamma Theta Phi 1st Annual Pole-Sitting and Raw Pig-a-Thon (Sponsored by Zeff's Auto Parts and WXLR 91 FM Golden Oldies Tower of Power Blast from Your Past Hot Hits), Bloomsburg State College, Greek Week Monster Blow-Out Bash 1992" plastered across your chest. Shirts like that confuse people in other countries. However, a discreet message affirming your concern for Gay Rainforest Whales would not be amiss and may even score points with a young Euro.

THOMAS NEENAN AND GREG HANCOCK

Learn or try to use the local language, even if only to say
"Thank you" and "Excuse me." Even learning the phrase "I love your
wonderful country" can get you a lot farther than "Why the hell
don't you wogs learn to speak English?"

ROBERT YOUNG PELTON

After warning against smoking in elevators and clapping in unison while getting drunk in bars, the *Overseas Safety Handbook* published by Japan's Foreign Ministry advises Japanese visitors to the U.S. that "it will be desirable that you refrain from making any racial comments in public."

Okay. You've taken a cab from the airport to your hotel, and the next day you learn from the porter that you paid about twenty-six times the going rate. That's natural. So you want a car. That's natural too. Two things to consider: First, just because a country has Avis doesn't mean it has gas. Second, take out the insurance. Running over a Bengali native is small potatoes, but hit someone's cow and you'll find yourself liable for about half the country's gross national product.

WILLIAM McGURN

If you are involved in an accident in Papua New Guinea, don't stop. Keep
going until you reach the nearest police station. There is a payback law by
which the wronged person randomly selects the next person matching your
skin color and kills him.

ERMA BOMBECK

It's important to understand that in the Third World most driving is done with the horn, or "Egyptian Brake Pedal," as it is known. There is a precise and complicated etiquette of horn use. Honk your horn only under the following circumstances:

1. When anything blocks the road.
2. When anything doesn't.
3. When anything might.
4. At red lights.
5. At green lights.
6. At all other times.

P. J. O'ROURKE

Most people have to discover this for themselves, but perhaps one or two people can be spared the embarrassment: That string over the shower in the European hotel is not the light cord. It's an emergency bell. If you pull it, people will be along when you least want them.

BETSY WADE

In an underdeveloped country, don't drink the water; in a developed country, don't breathe the air.

ANONYMOUS

Never take a cold bath in Africa, unless ordered to do so by a doctor.

WILLIAM HENRY CROSS

If you need to use a medical facility, keep in mind all emergency medical care is free of charge in Latvia—don't let any medical personnel tell you otherwise. However, you will probably receive better service if you slip tips to all those who help you: Doctors, nurses and orderlies.

INARA ASTRIDA PUNGA AND WILLIAM HOUGH

The best travel tip I can pass on to you is don't. Stay at home—it's nicer.
If someone says you must travel, get them to buy the ticket. Never pay the
full fare. Take a box of your own food: Freshly cooked chicken or salmon,
some perfect fruit and your favorite cheese. Take a calculator so you can
work out how much extra you'd be paying per hour to sit somewhere
up front where it is almost as hellish as it is back here.

LEN DEIGHTON

Dress impressively like the French, speak with authority like the Germans,
have blond hair like the Scandinavians, and speak of no American presidents
except Lincoln, Roosevelt and Kennedy.

SYLVAINE ROUY NEVES

Never go on trips with anyone you do not love.

ERNEST HEMINGWAY

Avoid any place you've ever heard of.

ARTHUR FROMMER

Grin like a dog and wander aimlessly.

PAUL THEROUX

TRAVELING COMPANIONS

The most common of all antagonisms arises from a man's taking a seat beside you on the train, a seat to which he is completely entitled.

ROBERT BENCHLEY

Sociability has an inverse relation to density. It is a law of airline travel . . . that two passengers separated by an empty seat will get into a conversation, but three passengers packed in a single row will not say a word to one another for the whole flight.

LOUIS MENAND

Whenever I travel I like to keep the seat next to me empty. I found a great way to do it. When someone walks down the aisle and says to you, "Is someone sitting there?" just say, "No one—except the Lord."

CAROL LEIFER

If you're traveling alone, beware of seatmates who by way of starting a conversation make remarks like: "I just have to talk to someone—my teeth are spying on me" or "Did you know that squirrels are the devil's ovenmits?"

MISS PIGGY

Except for the Rothschilds and madmen, all first-class passengers travel on expense accounts.

RUSSELL BAKER

In America there are two classes of travel: First Class and with children.

ROBERT BENCHLEY

More children are flying now than ever before because it's cheaper for a mother to travel with her kids than put them in a day-care center. Most of the

mothers you see on planes have no particular destination in mind and are just killing time until their husbands can take them to Burger Chef for dinner.

ART BUCHWALD

Traveling with three kids and dragging a trailer behind us wasn't the swiftest thing we ever did. In retrospect, I should never have given birth to more children than we had car windows.

ERMA BOMBECK

As you board the plane, you should be able to locate your seat by following the sound of the complimentary howling children, conveniently placed within strangling range on either side of your seat. (Remember, in case of emergency, place the oxygen mask on *yourself* first, and *then* strangle the howling children.)

CHRIS HARRIS

It's easier to find a traveling companion than to get rid of one.

ART BUCHWALD

VISITORS

Fish and visitors stink in three days.
BENJAMIN FRANKLIN

The American novelist Jacqueline Susann was a guest at Maurice Chevalier's country home, where the meals were well prepared and elegantly presented but the portions were small. When after dinner one evening the host asked Miss Susann what she would like to drink, she replied, "Maurice, I never drink on an empty stomach."

The only thing as draining as having a house guest is being one. In your effort not to be any trouble, you do twice as much housework as you ever do at home, and still your hosts' faces grow longer and longer as they knock themselves out trying to be cheerful. And this is assuming that they don't have a convertible sofa designed by a chiropractor who wants to increase business, or an un-housebroken but amorous dog. Being a house guest might be fun if you had a good experience in the Army, or if you come from a large family. But otherwise. . . .

MARGO KAUFMAN

Oscar Levant was a long-term guest at the home of the George S. Kaufmans. At the end of one of his visits, Mrs. Kaufman told him that she had tipped each of the servants three dollars and told them it was from Levant. "Three dollars?" Levant replied. "Give them five—otherwise they'll think I'm stingy!"

FOREIGNERS

Americans

There is no such thing as an American. They are all exiles, uprooted,
transplanted and doomed to sterility.

EVELYN WAUGH

Americans are the only people in the world known to me whose status
anxiety prompts them to advertise their college and university affiliations in
the rear window of their automobiles.

PAUL FUSSELL

Americans are like a rich father who wishes he knew how to give his
son the hardships that made him rich.

ROBERT FROST

Americans are rather partial to food.
You will be struck by the number of overweight people.

U.S.A.: Est et Sud (Guides Bleus)

Americans can eat garbage, provided you sprinkle it liberally with ketchup,
mustard, chili sauce, Tabasco sauce, cayenne pepper, or any other
condiment which destroys the original flavor of the dish.

HENRY MILLER

When you consider how indifferent Americans are to the quality
and cooking of the food they put into their insides, it cannot but strike
you as peculiar that they should take such pride in the mechanical
appliances they use for its excretion.

W. SOMERSET MAUGHAM

The genius of you Americans is that you never make clear-cut stupid moves, only complicated stupid moves which make us wonder at the possibility that there may be something to them which we are missing.

GAMAL ABDEL NASSER

I have defined the 100% American as 99% an idiot. And they just adore me.

GEORGE BERNARD SHAW

Americans are broad-minded people. They'll accept the fact that a person can be an alcoholic, a dope fiend, a wife beater, and even a newspaperman, but if a man doesn't drive there's something wrong with him.

ART BUCHWALD

The Americans are a queer people; they can't rest.

STEPHEN LEACOCK

Americans who travel abroad for the first time are often shocked to discover that, despite all the progress that has been made in the last 30 years, many foreign people still speak in foreign languages.

DAVE BARRY

Americans are desperate to escape crime, pollution, noise, rudeness, and traffic jams—*i.e.,* people. Once they move somewhere new to get away from people, they discover they are hated by people who hate people who are trying to get away from people they hate.

FLORENCE KING

Argentines

An Argentine is an Italian who speaks Spanish, thinks he's French, but would like to be English.

OLD SAYING

Australians

[Australians are] violently loud alcoholic roughnecks whose idea of
fun is to throw up on your car. The national sport is breaking furniture and
the average daily consumption of beer in Sydney is ten and three quarters
Imperial gallons for children under the age of nine.

P. J. O'ROURKE

Californians

Californians invented the concept of life-style.
This alone warrants their doom.

DON DELILLO

Californians go into ecstasies over what they refrain from eating.

QUENTIN CRISP

The only thing Californians read is the license plate in front of them.

NEIL SIMON

Canadians

Canadians carry the burden of being widely regarded as the
most boring people in the world. Perhaps this is partly because of the
spreading of the poisoned testimony of their neighbors. The reputation of
the most respectable person might be sullied by the accident of living next
door to a malevolent gossip. And Canada undoubtedly suffered from the
geographical equivalent of a bigoted bitch across the garden fence.

MARK LAWSON

A Canadian is just like an American. Only without the gun.

DAVE FOLEY

Danes

From Hamlet to Kierkegaard, the word "Danish" has been synonymous
with fun, fun, fun. . . . Who else would have the sense of humor to stuff prunes
and toe cheese into lumps of wet dough and serve it to you for breakfast? . . .
Let's hear it for those very wonderful kooky, very crazy, very wacky, very
witty Danes! They're the *living end.* And vice versa.

TONY HENDRA

Egyptians

I can't think much of a people who drew cats the same way
for four thousand years.

LORD KITCHENER

The English

The Englishman has all the qualities of a poker except its occasional warmth.

DANIEL O'CONNELL

Sheep with a nasty side.

CYRIL CONNOLLY

It is said of an Englishman that he hanged himself to avoid
the daily task of dressing and undressing.

JOHANN WOLFGANG VON GOETHE

The most dangerous thing in the world is to make a friend
of an Englishman, because he'll come sleep in your closet rather
than spend ten shillings on a hotel.

TRUMAN CAPOTE

The national sport of England is obstacle racing. People fill
their rooms with useless and cumbersome furniture, and spend the
rest of their lives trying to dodge it.

HERBERT BEERBOHM TREE

The English think soap is civilization.

HEINRICH VON TREITSCHKE

The English find ill-health not only interesting but respectable and
often experience death in the effort to avoid a fuss.

PAMELA FRANKAU

No one can be as calculatedly rude as the British,
which amazes Americans, who do not understand studied insult
and can only offer abuse as a substitute.

PAUL GALLICO

The English never smash a face. They merely refrain from asking it to dinner.

MARGARET HALSEY

The Englishman, even if he is alone, forms an orderly queue of one.

GEORGE MIKES

The English think incompetence is the same thing as sincerity.

QUENTIN CRISP

Contrary to popular belief, English women do not wear tweed nightgowns.

HERMIONE GINGOLD

The German originates it, the Frenchman imitates it, the Englishman exploits it.

GERMAN SAYING

The French

I would have loved [France]—without the French.

D. H. LAWRENCE

Frenchmen are like gunpowder, each by itself smutty and contemptible, but mass them together and they are terrible indeed!

SAMUEL TAYLOR COLERIDGE

Ever want to slap an entire country?

STEVE LANDESBERG

They aren't much at fighting wars anymore. Despite their reputation for fashion, their women have spindly legs. Their music is sappy. But they do know how to whip up a plate of grub.

MIKE ROYKO

Oh, how I love humanity
With love so pure and pringlish
And how I hate the horrid French
Who never will be English.

G. K. CHESTERTON

"What is the difference between heaven and hell?" the wise man was asked. "In heaven," he replied, "the English are the police, the French are the cooks, the Italians are the lovers, the Swiss are the administrators, and the Germans are the mechanics. Whereas in hell, the English are the cooks, the French are the administrators, the Italians are the mechanics, the Swiss are the lovers, and the Germans are the police."

The simple thing is to consider the French as an erratic and brilliant people . . . who have all the gifts except that of running their country.
JAMES CAMERON

They are a short, blue-vested people who
carry their own onions when cycling abroad, and have a yard
which is 3.37 inches longer than other people's.
ALAN COREN

The French are sawed-off sissies who eat snails and slugs and cheese that smells like people's feet. Utter cowards who force their own children to drink wine, they gibber like baboons even when you try to speak to them in their own wimpy language.
P. J. O'ROURKE

These people *needed* to invent perfume.
DENNIS MILLER

Cheese-eatin' surrender monkeys.
The Simpsons

Germans

The Germans are very seldom troubled with any extraordinary ebullience or effervescences of wit, and it is not prudent to try it upon them.

LORD CHESTERFIELD

The German people are an orderly, vain, deeply sentimental, and rather insensitive people. They seem to feel at their best when they are singing in chorus, saluting, or obeying orders.

H. G. WELLS

Germans are split into two broad categories: those with tall spikes on their hats, and those with briefcases. Up until 1945, the country's history was made by those with spikes. After 1945, it was made by those with briefcases.

ALAN COREN

They are a fine people but quick to catch the disease of anti-humanity. I think it's because of their poor elimination. Germany is a headquarters for constipation.

GEORGE GROSZ

One thing I will say for the Germans, they are always perfectly willing to give somebody else's land to somebody else.

WILL ROGERS

Greeks

The Greeks: Dirty and impoverished descendants of a bunch of
la-de-da fruit salads who invented democracy and then forgot how to use it
while walking around dressed up like girls.

P. J. O'ROURKE

Hungarians

Hungarians form not only a local clique but also a world-wide
conspiracy, third in importance only to homosexuals and Roman Catholics.
A homosexual Roman Catholic Hungarian cannot possibly have a worry in
the world, he will fall on his feet wherever he may find himself.

GEORGE MIKES

The Hungarian-born physicist Leo Szilard was debating the possibility of
intelligent extraterrestrial life with his colleague Enrico Fermi, who enu-
merated all the circumstantial evidence in its favor: The vast numbers of
stars with presumed planetary systems and the likelihood that at least some
of them would have residents capable of interplanetary travel. "Yet," Fermi
asked, "Why haven't they visited Earth yet?"

"They're already here," replied Szilard, "only they call themselves
Hungarians."

Indians

It is a curious people. With them, all life seems to be
sacred except human life.

MARK TWAIN

Indians love to reduce the prosaic to the mystic.
JAN MORRIS

Being Hindu means never having to say you're sorry.
GITA MEHTA

The Irish

Charming, soft-voiced, quarrelsome, priest-ridden, feckless, and happily devoid of the slightest integrity in our stodgy English sense of the word.
NOËL COWARD

A nation of brilliant failures, the Irish, who are too poetical to be poets.
MAX BEERBOHM

The English and Americans dislike only *some* Irish—the same Irish that the Irish themselves detest, Irish writers—the ones that *think*.
BRENDAN BEHAN

An Irish queer is a fellow who prefers women to drink.
SEAN O'FAOLAIN

The Irish are a fair people; they never speak well of one another.
SAMUEL JOHNSON

The Japanese

The Japanese have perfected good manners and made them
indistinguishable from rudeness.

PAUL THEROUX

The Japanese tend to communicate via nuance and euphemism, often
leaving important things unsaid; whereas Americans tend to think they're
being subtle when they refrain from grabbing the listener by the shirt.

DAVE BARRY

Koreans

The Koreans have been called "The Irish of the East,"
but this is an insult to the Irish.

JAMES KIRKUP

Neopolitans

Neapolitans, especially when exiled to the north of Italy, give themselves airs
solely on the strength of their origin. They will sometimes even apologize for
being in Cremona or Padua, as though they have let the Neapolitan side
down. Civic pride is a substitute for talent, probably vocal. They will sing,
usually badly, at the drop of a hat.

ANTHONY BURGESS

New Yorkers

The faces in New York remind me of people who played a game and lost.

MURRAY KEMPTON

What the New Yorker calls home would seem like a couple of closets
to most Americans, yet he manages not only to live there but also to grow
trees and cockroaches right on the premises.

RUSSELL BAKER

New York: The only city where people make radio requests like,
"This is for Tina—I'm sorry I stabbed you."

CAROL LEIFER

It is one of the prime provincialities of New York that its inhabitants
lap up trivial gossip about essential nobodies they've never set eyes on, while
continuing to boast that they could live somewhere for twenty years without
so much as exchanging pleasantries with their neighbors across the hall.

LOUIS KRONENBERGER

New Yorkers like to boast that if you can survive in New York, you can survive
anywhere. But if you can survive anywhere, why live in New York?

EDWARD ABBEY

Nigerians

In the beginning God created the Universe. Then He created the moon,
the stars and the wild beasts of the forests. On the sixth day he created the
Nigerian. But on the seventh day while God rested, the Nigerian invented noise.

ANTHONY ENAHORO

Poles

There are few virtues which the Poles do not possess and there are
few errors they have ever avoided.

WINSTON CHURCHILL

Provençals

When a Provençal looks you in the eye and tells you that he will be hammering on your door ready to start work next Tuesday . . . the behavior of his hands is all-important. If they are still, or patting you reassuringly on the arm, you can expect him on Tuesday. If one hand is held out at waist height, palm downwards, and begins to rock from side to side, adjust the timetable to Wednesday or Thursday. If the rocking develops into an agitated waggle, he's really talking about next week or God knows when, depending on circumstances beyond his control.

PETER MAYLE

Russians

One Russian is an anarchist
Two Russians are a chess game
Three Russians are a revolution
Four Russians are the Budapest String Quartet.

JASCHA HEIFETZ

Scots

It is never difficult to distinguish between a Scotsman with a
grievance and a ray of sunshine.

P. G. WODEHOUSE

The Scots do make good whiskey. In Bobby Burns, they had a great poet,
but I've never drunk enough whiskey to understand him.

DONALD McCAIG

No McTavish
Was ever lavish.
OGDEN NASH

Serbs

A gang of brutal yokels with a cultural life only marginally richer than
that of Neanderthal man.
JOHN NAUGHTON

Southerners

Southerners are probably not more hospitable than
New Englanders are; they are simply more willing to remind you of
the fact that they are being hospitable.
RAY L. BIRDWHISTELL

Spaniards

The most cohesive and mutually abrasive nationality.
RICHARD EDER

Swedes

Long before I visited Sweden for the first time, I had built up a composite
portrait of the average Swede. He was withdrawn and spasmodic, reserved on
the surface but explosive beneath it, veering between troughs of depression
and fits of abandon. He was a pacifist, a socialist, an alcoholic and a hiker. He
swam nude and tended to commit suicide during the long winters. Like many
other popular misconceptions (e.g., that the French are greedy and the Spanish stoical), this turned out to be fairly close to the truth.
KENNETH TYNAN

The Swiss

The Swiss are not a people so much as a neat, clean, quite solvent business.

WILLIAM FAULKNER

The only nation I've ever been tempted to feel really
racist about are the Swiss—a whole country of phobic handwashers
living in a giant Barclays Bank.

JONATHAN RABAN

Every time I arrive in the country, I'm reminded of the old joke about God creating Switzerland. God asked the Swiss people what they wanted in the way of a country. They said they wanted huge Alps, deafening streams, and beautiful pastures where their riotous cows could ring their disco bells through the night. God provided all this in three days. The first Swiss innkeeper was so pleased, he asked if there was something he could do for God in return. God said yes, as a matter of fact. He was a little thirsty. He would like a glass of milk. "Fine," said the innkeeper. "That will be ten francs."

DAN JENKINS

Tahitians

I never saw a people that seemed so hopelessly bored as the Tahitians.

HENRY ADAMS

Texans

Texans do not talk like other Americans. They drawl, twang, or sound like the Frito Bandito, only not jolly. *Shit* is a three-syllable word with a *y* in it.

MOLLY IVINS

THINGS YOU WOULD *Never* HEAR A REAL TEXAN SAY:

I think that song needs more French horn.
The tires on that truck are too big.
There's no place in my home for obscenity!
I believe the proper word is "African-American."
I'll have the decaf latté, please.
William Robert, you appall me.
This red wine has a rather cheeky bouquet.
I've got two cases of Perrier for the Super Bowl.
Fried pig rinds are disgusting.
You're watching football? Change the channel—*Oprah* is on!
Duct tape won't fix that.
Come to think of it, I'll have a Heineken.
We don't keep firearms in this house.
You can't feed that to the dog.
I thought Graceland was tacky.
No kids in the back of the pickup—it's just not safe.
Wrestling is not real.

KINKY FRIEDMAN

Tibetans

It was . . . against Tibetan social usage, at least among the proletariat, to wash at any time between birth and death, a decision readily understandable in a people who live in conditions of such climactic acerbity, but one which nevertheless tended to make their company oppressive.

JAMES CAMERON

Turks

It would seem from their history that the three basic elements in the Turkish national character are cruelty, courage, and inefficiency.

SIMON RAVEN

ACCOMMODATIONS

To the man traveling alone, his hotel room, first entered in rumpled clothes, with a head light from sleeplessness, looms as the arena where he will suffer insomnia, constipation, loneliness, nightmares, and telephone calls: his room will be woven into the deeper, less comfortable self that travel uncovers.

JOHN UPDIKE

I seem to spend half my life arriving at strange hotels. And asking if I may go to bed immediately.

"And would you mind filling the hot water bottle? . . . Thank you that was delicious. No, I shan't require anything more."

The strange door shuts upon the stranger, and then I slip down in the sheets. Waiting for the shadows to come out of the corners and spin their slow, slow webs over the Ugliest Wallpaper of All.

KATHERINE MANSFIELD

As the crowded joyous ferry-boat was nearing Messina, I was seized by an ailment perhaps confined to myself and which I have isolated and named. I call it "Xenodochiophobia." It makes me sweat with anxiety about what I shall find in the hotel that I approach. If the room should be of the wrong shape, too high or too low, too narrow, with furniture out of proportion, dusty, grimy, with torn wallpapers, without a reading lamp by the bed, without a wastepaper basket, I know I shall feel utterly miserable in it.

My fears with regard to the hotel here at Messina were not groundless. Entrance hall magnificent with double grand staircase leading up to rooms I shall not praise, and the price charged for them is not in proportion to the rooms but to the splendor of the staircase.

BERNARD BERENSON

Before the days of the Hyatts, Holiday Inns, Marriotts, Howard Johnsons, Ramada Inns, and the like, American hotels used to range from bad to fair.

But now, they are almost uniformly BAD. The reason is their grandiloquence, their fondness for putting on airs that don't at all become them. Like "turndown service," the mention of which in its publicity one hotel hopes will occasion a stampede toward its registration desk. Turndown service: that means that between 6:00 and 10:00 P.M. an employee will open *and turn down* your top bedsheet, with attendant blanket. And not just that: She (he? Not really plausible) will also deposit two, and sometimes three, individually wrapped *candies* on the turndown. This is what hotel publicity means when it invokes its favorite magic word, *luxury.*

PAUL FUSSELL

Generally speaking, the length and grandness of a hotel's name are an exact opposite reflection of its quality. Thus the Hotel Central will prove to be a clean, pleasant place in a good part of town, and the Hotel Royal Majestic-Fantastic will be a fleabag next to a topless bowling alley.

MISS PIGGY

The cottage [in Oxfordshire] was thatched. It was also smack up against the road. The road turned out to be a major traffic artery. Open the cottage door, venture out an inch, a truck (lorry) would take off your nose. Inside it was dark and musty, overfull with dour furniture and dingy doilies, except for the kitchen, which was furnished completely in white plastic. A huge pay phone dominated the living room. There was a stench of mildew, a truly perilous staircase, a dying spider flailing in the bath. The carpeting alone could cause suicide.

I stayed one night, long enough to find out the cottage was in the flight path for a nearby R.A.F. base.

CYNTHIA HEIMEL

No pudding, and no fun.
QUEEN VICTORIA, *of a Scottish inn*

Catherine and I had rented the house in East Flanders unseen. When we walked through the front door we knew straight away it had been a mistake. The interiors of Belgian houses are often dark, as if some rogue troglodyte gene were still loose in the land, but this one was positively Stygian. The walls were covered in brown velvet. The curtains were the color of Franciscan robes. All the wood had been stained a somber shade of mahogany. If the carpet pattern had a name, it was probably "Swamp Thing."

The room was decorated with religious icons and medieval weaponry. . . . On the roof-beams spiders waged war for the last square inch of *lebensraum.* Switching on the lights made little difference. The brown walls sucked in brightness and burped back dust. It was the only living-room I have ever been in that would have been cheered up by the presence of a few bats.

If the lounge was *The Addams Family,* the kitchen was strictly *The Young Ones.* There was rat poison next to the tea-towels. In the fridge an open jar of béarnaise sauce was so far past its sell-by date the bacteria in it had evolved to the stage where it was capable of hot-wiring a Ford Escort. The grease on the cutlery was sufficient to lubricate a combine harvester. Extended families of dark beetles eyed us reproachfully from the saucepans whenever we mentioned cooking.

HARRY PEARSON

Our hotel [in Bali] was so authentic that it sat in the rice fields with its soaring thatched roof, its woven-grass half walls, and . . . nothing. It was, in fact, a porch. Let us call it a sleeping pavilion. It was an extremely hot, open-air, sleeping pavilion with no fan to move the equatorial air, and no mosquito netting. And we had paid for a long stay in advance.

JUDITH GREBER

It was in a teak forest in northern Thailand. I hadn't been able to find anywhere to stay and it was late so when I saw the hotel I had to stay there. It turned out to be a hotel-cum-nightclub-cum-knocking shop. There were no proper rooms, just "assignment cabins" made of corrugated iron for clients to take prostitutes. It was filthy. There was just a bed in the cabin and the sheets on it were crunchy with body fluids. There was nowhere to hang your clothes and it was full of mosquitoes. I couldn't face lying on the bed, so I pushed it against the door so that no one could get in. I spent the whole night leaning against the cast-iron wall getting attacked by mosquitoes and thinking, "What am I doing here?" The bathroom was a stinking hole in the floor and a plastic tub full of stagnant water. I spent the night listening to shouting and the Thai strip-club music.

LISA ST. AUBIN DE TERAN

As for the *loesmans,* or "guest houses," [in Jogjakarta] where the pedal cabbies took us, they were no more than designated corners of those sprawling atriums in which the Indonesians sat out lifetimes with a minimum of disturbance. The inns' plaster dividers made a gallery for pin-ups of American rock groups who were vapid enough for export: the Spiral Staircase, Suzi Quatro. Masons' mishaps let in malarial mosquitoes like the *Titanic* let in water. A nail driven into the wall served as a closet. Sheets? Sometimes washed, always stained. Telephones? The whole province was lucky to have one. Brotherhood was the only item in great supply, which wasn't so bad, except that the main time it got called into action was over the toilet, the squatter, the flushless hole—where guests learned to love the look of the next guy's worm-riddled feces as they loved their own. And when hotels down the road beckoned us with flyers promising "MUSIC IN EVERY ROOM" we were amazed when a single radio rasped in the common courtyard.

JOHN KRICH

We booked into the local five-star hotel [in Urfa, Turkey], the only cara-
vansary in town as it happened. The rooms were the size of a large closet.
The beds were Indian rope charpoy style—great for bad backs. But it was the
plumbing system that was the most captivating aspect of the place. The
clientele was all male and the "rooms" were arranged in a long line on one
floor. At the rear of each was a "V" shaped trough which ran at a descending
angle along the entire line of rooms. A trickle of water ran through it and the
guests were invited, in case of need, to contribute to that water flow. I dozed
off to the symphony of over-full Turkish bladders splashing out the evening's
harvest into the trough a few doors upstream from my room.

LARRY COLLINS

We shared a room [in a Turkish hotel] with a Belgian couple.
My sheet was littered with the hairs and scent of the previous occupant.
When I complained about my dirty linen to the hotel man he
immediately rushed up, apologized, and turned it over.

RICK STEVES

It was a nightmare room [in Istanbul], the room of a drug fiend or a miscre-
ant or perhaps both. It was illuminated by a forty-watt bulb and looked out
on a black wall with something slimy growing on it. The bed was a fearful thing,
almost perfectly concave. Underneath it was a pair of cloth-topped boots.
The sheets were almost clean but on them was the unmistakable impress of a
human form and they were still warm. In the corner there was a wash basin
with one long red hair in it and a tap which leaked. Somewhere nearby a fun-
fair was testing its loud-hailing apparatus, warming up for a night of revelry.

ERIC NEWBY

Behind the door to [room] 1414 [in the Ishtar Hotel, Baghdad] lay a chamber
that gave the distinct impression of having been submerged in stagnant
water for several months and then kiln-dried. The only functioning light was
a terrifying five-foot column containing several fluorescent tubes that sucked

what little color was left in the floor, furniture, and walls into a throbbing sheen of raw electricity. Something or someone had been slaughtered at the foot of the bed, judging by a vast magenta stain. A very big cigar had once been allowed to incinerate itself on top of the television, leaving an inch-deep trench in the plastic casing. Above the bath was a jagged hole in the ceiling large enough for a man to climb through. Slabs and shards of plaster still lay in the tub. And deep within a multi-hued blizzard, believe it or not, Disney's *Aladdin* was actually playing on the only TV channel I could find.

PAUL WILLIAM ROBERTS

The [Bulgarian] hotel was so bad that when we walked in, my wife and I burst out laughing. . . . The toilet was all concrete—a concrete block with a stainless steel toilet and a big flower-shaped shower head of stainless steel and you practically had to stand on the pan to get washed. We were there a week—a week too long—and we spent three days in the room because of the rain. The only good thing was I saw a hummingbird there—that was the only good thing about Bulgaria.

DES DILLON

Nothing like the Russian hotel experience.
Hookers and the armed men who protect them.

HENRY ROLLINS

I once stayed in an airport hotel in New Jersey. It was night when I got to my room and I was amazed by the bolts and chains and the amount of security notices on the back of the door. I went to bed but, as I was falling asleep, the telephone rang. I picked it up and the voice on the end of the line said, "Is Joey there?" I said "no" but he said, "Tell him I'm coming up. He's going to get it." I stayed awake worrying all night.

LOYD GROSSMAN

Staying in any of the chain motels beside the Interstate
is like being sprayed lightly with Lysol, sealed in Tupperware and
stashed in the refrigerator for the night.

LANCE MORROW

It's possible to drive from here to California and stay at
more or less the same motel the entire way.

IAN FRAZIER

We stayed at Caesar's Palace, a giant hotel-casino authentically
decorated to look exactly the way the Roman Empire would have looked
if it had consisted mainly of slot machines.

DAVE BARRY

We checked into the Overdose Suite at the De Franco Hotel on Sunset [in
Hollywood]. The Scene of the Crime: A white stucco ceiling, strange stains
on the carpet, peeling wallpaper, a dead fish tank set into the wall, a crushed
can of soda spilling thick residue in the bottom of the fridge, huge mirrors so
you can watch yourself suck or blow or get sucked or blowed, a suicide balcony that plummets straight down to where your chalk outline will be drawn
opposite the House of Blues, next door to the Comedy Store, just down the
road from the Marlboro Man. Roy Rogers used to live here—with Trigger.

SEAN CONDON

In some hotels they give you a little sewing kit.
You know what I do? I sew the towels together. One time I sewed
a button on a lampshade. I like to leave a mark.

GEORGE CARLIN

STATIONERY CURMUDGEON

I don't steal towels from great hotels any more. I steal notepaper. But only if it displays the hotel's insignia. I have no need of plain writing paper, just as I never had need of plain towels. The reason why one steals notepaper (or towels) from great hotels is to perpetuate the memory of a rare and ennobling experience—which is what a great hotel should be. If I didn't have an ennobling experience, I would leave their notepaper and towels behind. So the theft is a compliment, and should be taken in that spirit.

DAVID DALE

I have thousands of little shampoos from thousands
of hotels and I don't even have hair.
JERRY DELLA FEMINA

Twenty-four-hour room service generally refers to the length of time that it
takes for the club sandwich to arrive. This is indeed disheartening,
particularly when you've ordered scrambled eggs.
FRAN LEBOWITZ

I spent the night at the [Winnipeg] Downtowner Inn, a motel intriguingly
reminiscent of a mobile home. It was one of those establishments in which,
as protection against theft or absentmindedness, the key was attached to a
vast slab of aluminum, so cumbersome that only guests with a tin leg or a
permanent erection could plausibly forget they had it in their pocket.
MARK LAWSON

As for hostels, you get what you pay for, and if you're paying two bucks a
night don't be surprised to find yourself sharing a bed with the keeper's
syphilitic son and a descendant of every insect who made it onto Noah's Ark.
WILLIAM MCGURN

THE FOOD

If you can't see water, don't order fish.
ANONYMOUS

Eat lettuce [in Mexico] only if sterilized by a blowtorch.
BENJAMIN KEAN

Never eat in a restaurant that features men in sombreros.
THOMAS SWICK

Greek food is always better outside Greece than inside it.
DAVID DALE

HOW TO USE CHOPSTICKS

Take one chopstick and place it between the base of your thumb and your hand, extending outward between your middle and ring fingers. Grasp the other chopstick with the tips of your thumb and index finger. Now, holding the two sticks parallel, raise them over your head and signal to the waiter that you would like him to please bring you a fork.

DAVE BARRY

Mongolian Travel Survival Tip No. 1 is "Always carry a bottle of chili sauce," because the food in Mongolia is, well, bloody awful; gastronomic purgatory. Almost every meal outside of UB [the capital city of Ulaanbaatar], in a restaurant or home, is a choice of either boiled or fried mutton . . . and the more fat, the better. Liberal doses of spicy sauce can hide the texture and taste of mutton, and help the lumpy, fatty and hairy bits slide down the throat. The smell and taste of mutton seems to permeate everything. Biscuits, soap and even the local currency smell, and it took several weeks to get rid of the mutton smell from my body after I returned home (where the smell of boiled fatty mutton is not cherished).

PAUL GREENWAY

Never eat Chinese food in Oklahoma.

BRYAN MILLER

You can travel 50 thousand miles in America without once tasting a piece of good bread.

HENRY MILLER

You can find your way across this country using burger joints the way a navigator uses stars. We have munched Bridge burgers in the shadow of the Brooklyn Bridge and Cable burgers hard by the Golden Gate, Dixie burgers in the sunny South and Yankee Doodle burgers in the North. . . . We had a Capitol burger—guess where. And so help us, in the inner courtyard of the Pentagon, a Penta burger.

CHARLES KURALT

The Russian tourist in America is instructed to ask for the following in restaurants: "Please give me curds, sower cream, fried chicks, pulled bread and one jellyfish."

The Russian-English Phrasebook

[Advice to Russians visiting the United States:] Never refuse anything that is offered. Over here, people offer only once. Let's examine a specific situation. You are about to take a stroll, and your host offers you some sandwiches and a can of Pepsi. Take them. When hunger strikes, you will not find anything edible for less than a dollar, except for fruit. Who can survive solely on fruit? Please note that all Americans eat sandwiches for lunch and that they sit on any available surface, including sidewalks. Do not hesitate to plop down while eating.

VIKTOR VIKTOROV

Just as in Mexico food is peppered to excess, so in New York all drinks are over-iced. Ice is as much an obsession to the Americans as curry to the Indians. One cannot but feel an overt sympathy for the old man on the baby's highchair who thus for forty years must have been corroding his alimentary canal and stomach. The helpless gut suffers, unheeded and unfelt, for the momentary pleasure during which the frost passes into the throat.

CECIL BEATON

In England there are sixty different religions, but only one sauce.

VOLTAIRE

English cuisine is generally so threadbare that for years there has been a gentleman's agreement in the civilized world to allow the Brits preeminence in the matter of tea—which, after all, comes down to little more than the ability to boil water.

WILFRID SHEED

The average cooking in the average hotel for the average Englishman explains to a large extent the English bleakness and taciturnity. Nobody can beam and warble while chewing pressed beef smeared with diabolical mustard. Nobody can exult aloud while ungluing from his teeth a quivering tapioca pudding.

KAREL CAPEK

Even today, well-brought-up English girls are taught by their mothers to boil all veggies for at least a month and a half, just in case one of the dinner guests turns up without his teeth.

CALVIN TRILLIN

Oats: A grain, which in England is generally given to horses,
but in Scotland supports the people.

SAMUEL JOHNSON

When's the last time you went out for Canadian food?

MIKE MEYERS

SIMPLY INDIGESTIBLE

Airag (Asia) A drink made from fermented mare's milk by nomadic
Mongolian herdsmen.

Ant Eggs (Mexico)

Balut (Philippines) Partially-incubated duck egg (nascent bones and
feathers provide the crunchiness).

Cow's Udders (Latin America) Grilled.

Fire Ant Soup (Laos)

Haggis (Scotland) Sheep's stomach filled with a mixture of the animal's
minced heart, liver, and lungs, and boiled with suet, onions, oatmeal,
and Scotch.

Jackfruit (India, Southeast Asia) An enormous relative of the breadfruit
that emits an overpowering stench when ripe (not a deterrent to its
devotees, who bring them on busses).

Monkey (West Africa) Barbecued.

Pickled Duck Tongue (Taiwan)

Pig's Blood Soup (Poland)

Spotted Dick (England) Steamed or boiled pudding shaped in a roll.

Vegemite (Australia) A salty yeast preparation adored by millions of
Aussies who consider it a national treasure, and despised by millions of
visitors who consider it a national psychosis.

As we approached the food that had been laid out on the buffet tables [in our hotel in Barbados], it occurred to me that if the sons of lieutenant colonels in the Coldstream Guards had bar mitzvahs, this is what the reception spread would look like. The display reflected the extraordinary care the English have always taken with the appearance of special-occasion victuals; their interest in food tends to peak just before the eating.

CALVIN TRILLIN

France has found a unique way of controlling its unwanted critter population. They have done this by giving animals like snails, pigeons, and frogs fancy names, thus transforming common backyard pests into expensive delicacies. These are then served to gullible tourists, who will eat anything they can't pronounce; the French could serve *la wadde du gum à la sidewalk* and folks would still gobble it up.

CHRIS HARRIS

It is not a figure of speech, it is a mere statement of fact to say that a French cook will spit in the soup—that is, if he is not going to drink it himself. He is an artist, but his art is not cleanliness. To a certain extent he is even dirty because he is an artist, for food, to look smart, needs dirty treatment. When a steak, for instance, is brought up for the head cook's inspection, he does not handle it with a fork. He picks it up in his fingers and slaps it down, runs his thumb round the dish and licks it to taste the gravy, runs it round and licks again, then steps back and contemplates the piece of meat like an artist judging a picture, then presses it lovingly into place with his fat, pink fingers, every one of which he has licked a hundred times that morning. When he is satisfied, he takes a cloth and wipes his fingerprints from the dish, and hands it to the waiter. And the waiter, of course, dips his fingers into the gravy—his nasty, greasy fingers which he is forever running through his brilliantined hair.

GEORGE ORWELL

GUSTATORY DO'S AND DON'TS
AROUND THE WORLD

If you can't recognize what you're eating, wait until you finish before asking what it was. You'll enjoy it more.

At a Chinese table, fish is often served head, tail and all. The eyes are highly regarded by many. After the meal is eaten, just pick up the head and suck the eyes out. Tasty. Very tasty.

When in Australia or England, never say, "I'm stuffed." It has a highly sexual connotation.

The bold (or crazy) Japanese gourmand really does eat "Fugu," the toxic liver of the puffer fish. Specially trained and government-certified chefs prepare it in such a way that only a trace of the tetradotoxin remains to cause the mouth to tingle and the diner to know the thrill of dancing with Death. But sometimes Death decides to lead. The Japanese press reports about 300 such tangos per year. Cross this one off your dance card.

The most astonishing tropical fruit anywhere is the durian. A melon-like fruit with a yellow, pudding textured flesh, its odor is best described as pig shit, turpentine, and onions garnished with a dirty gym sock. It can be smelled from yards away. Despite its great local popularity, it is forbidden to eat durian on the subway in Singapore.

Anywhere in the South Pacific, refrain from talking of cannibalism. The popular term for human flesh is *long pig,* for its taste being similar to pork. If anyone should ever call you a *long pig,* get the hell outta Dodge.

RICHARD STERLING

I beg to offer the reader a formula I invented, which will teach him (should he ever come to Germany) what to expect. The simple rule is this: Let him taste the dish, and if it be not sour, he may be quite certain that it is greasy.

SIR F. B. HEAD

Think of the man who first tried German sausage.

JEROME K. JEROME

The food in Yugoslavia is either very good or very bad.
One day they served us fried chains.

MEL BROOKS

The food in Yugoslavia is fine if you like pork tartare.

ED BEGLEY, JR.

There is no question that Rumanian-Jewish food is heavy. One meal is equal in heaviness, I guess, to eight or nine years of steady mung-bean eating. Following the Rumanian tradition, garlic is used in excess to keep the vampires away; following the Jewish tradition, a dispenser of schmalz (liquid chicken fat) is kept on the table to give the vampires heartburn if they get through the garlic defense.

CALVIN TRILLIN

Rumanian-Yiddish cooking has killed more Jews than Hitler.

ZERO MOSTEL

CUSTOMS

Three hours behind schedule, our 747 finally lifted off for Los Angeles, where
U.S. customs officials confiscated a vacuum-sealed chorizo sausage I'd
purchased at the Madrid airport. But I wasn't upset in the least. With illicit
narcotics and AK-47 assault rifles pouring into the country, it was comforting
to know that our government has zero tolerance for souvenir chorizo.

JEFF KRAMER

Getting out of Pakistan was a normal Third World procedure.
A customs official explained the entire system of Pakistani tariff
regulation and passport control by rubbing his thumb against his forefinger.
"Fifty dollars," he said. I opened my wallet, foolishly revealing two
fifty-dollar bills. "One hundred dollars," he said.

P. J. O'ROURKE

A carton of cigarettes will ensure that you are speedily processed in most
African countries. A bottle of Johnny Walker will not get you far in a Muslim
country but will definitely expedite your exit visa in Colombia. Border cross-
ings in most Central American countries can be made for $100, and you can
drive as fast as you want in Mexico if you have a good supply of 20 dollar bills.
With such gifts, you may not need a visa entering a country and the customs
official may forgo even a cursory inspection of your vehicle.

ROBERT YOUNG PELTON

Madagascar is some different shit. The soldier/police at immigration had their patches safety-pinned onto their uniforms. I wonder if that's so they can tear them off when the insurrection happens. The guy at the visa counter haggled with me over how much to pay. He asked me what kind of currency I had. I told him I had some Kenyan, he said he wasn't interested. He asked me what else I had. I asked him what he would take. He listed dollars, German Marks, English Pounds, etc. I asked him how much in pounds. He said twenty. I told him I had ten. He said he'd take it.

HENRY ROLLINS

When a customs official asked Oscar Wilde if he had anything to declare upon his arrival in the United States, Wilde replied, "Nothing but my genius."

SOUVENIRS

What distinguishes the tourist [from the traveler] is the motives, few of which are ever openly revealed: to raise social status at home and to allay social anxiety; to realize fantasies of erotic freedom; and most important, to derive secret pleasure from posing momentarily as a member of a social class superior to one's own, to play the role of a "shopper" and spender whose life becomes significant and exciting only when one is exercising power by choosing what to buy.

PAUL FUSSELL

At a great American tourist attraction, the exit signs always lead you through the souvenir shop. This is good, because the souvenir shop is often more fun than the tourist attraction. . . . When Americans visit a true national shrine like Mount Rushmore, they like to commemorate this solemn experience by purchasing a T-shirt or a beach towel decorated with a cartoon that shows the naked butts of four men who are peering over the top of a mountain while one lost tourist is telling another, "As near as I can tell, we're somewhere behind Mount Rushmore."

PETER CARLSON

One of the drawbacks of going to Paris without the wife was the inevitable shopping list. When Billy Wilder embarked on such a trip, Mrs. Wilder asked him to send back some Charvet ties and a bidet. A few days after his arrival in the City of Light, he sent her the following message: "Charvet ties on way but impossible to obtain bidet. Suggest handstand in shower."

Our own part of the ship was not invaded by anybody, except one solitary figure. He was a man in European dress, with wistful eyes and a fine Hellenic face. Advancing to us with dignity, he asked us if we would buy what he called "special photographs." "Be off," said one of my friends. "Take the beastly things away." "Not beastly," he said gently, "academic." Then opening a leather case which he carried, he produced from its depths some polished cubes of olive wood, and with no change of manner except an increased gravity. "Perhaps," he went on, "you would like a piece of the true Cross."

W. H. MALLOCK

Inside [the shop in Khamir, Yemen], a man sprawled languidly across several burlap sacks, smoking a water pipe and grinning, like a fat Cheshire cat.

"I am Mohammed, at your service," he said, straightening his turban. "You want change money? You want sugar?" He paused. "You want bayonet?"

I smiled noncommittally. He opened a drawer. "These just in from Iran," he said, dropping a plump green grenade in my hand. "For you I make a special deal. Other villages, you find grenades only at Friday market. At Mohammed's every day."

TONY HORWITZ

I was walking on the beach [on Ko Phi Phi, an island off the southwestern coast of Thailand] when a boy with a gibbon on his shoulder grabbed my arm. "Wanna buy a ruby?" he asked. This wasn't my idea of a personal jeweler. The kid pulled out a box of precious stones. "Sapphire? Emerald? Diamond?"

MARGO KAUFMAN

PHOTO OPPORTUNITIES

No one wants to see your slides. Get that through your head. Not your parents
who gave you life. Not your kids who are insecure and need your approval. Not
your priest, minister, or rabbi who are paid to be kind and forgiving. Not even
someone whose life you saved in the war and who owes you big.

ERMA BOMBECK

Years ago, climbing the marble steps of the Acropolis, a companion
raised his camera to his eye and when the Parthenon came into view he
snapped it, before, as it were, he had seen it. This seemed to me the
placing of a barrier between himself and experience.

P. J. KAVANAGH

Travelers to a popular location, I thought, were like policemen or
the parents of missing children, wandering around with a photograph until
they got a match. Discovery was confirmation. The word "picturesque" had
achieved a new literality. It meant somewhere you had seen a picture of,
and to which you now traveled to take one of your own.

MARK LAWSON

My mother was a photographer. She snapped groups throughout my
childhood. There are tourists in my nightmares. That's how I know that they
are nightmares. Tourists are terrorists with cameras.

ANDREI CODRESCU

There is hardly a wall at the Captain Cook Hotel [on Christmas Island]
that does not exhibit a photograph of a foreigner, popeyed under the weight
of a potbellied, scaly, slack-jawed trophy—the mirror-image of its captor.

PAUL THEROUX

A large crowd was gathered around the pisser's plinth [the "Mannekin Pis," a famous statue in Brussels of a boy urinating] in the early morning, so that the scene resembled a shrine. The boy even wore a crown of flowers, like a urological Mother of God. The religious metaphor failed only with the faces of the congregation, which wore half-embarrassed smiles. Before taking a picture, people would wander around looking studiedly uninterested, as if they were pickpockets, before suddenly pulling up their cameras and stealing the scene. Then they would glance sideways and shrug, as if to indicate that *their* photography, if no one else's, was ironic or post-modernist.

MARK LAWSON

It wasn't the twelve busses a day that revved their motors in front of the house while tourists took pictures. It wasn't seeing our house [a landmark Victorian in San Francisco] pictured on the phone-book cover, shopping bags, postcards, plastic place mats, and sales brochures. It wasn't photographers shooting models on our doorstep without permission. What finally drove us out was being asked for our autographs because Clint Eastwood lived there in *The Dead Pool* and love trysts in *Tales of the City* took place on the park bench directly in front of the house. Strangers were so curious about the interior that they would ring our doorbell and ask to be invited in as if it were a movie set. We were a shooting gallery for shutterbugs.

BARBARA BLADEN

What do you get when you take pictures anyway? The chance to freeze dry your friends with boredom? The opportunity to watch the sunset over the Gulf of Messenia, alone, while your mate shimmies up a balcony to get a shot without intruding telephone wires?

MARGO KAUFMAN

GOING ABROAD

The Europeans can't figure out what side of the road to drive on, and I can't figure out how to flush their toilets. Do I push the knob or pull it or twist it or pump it? And I keep cracking my shins on that bidet thing. (Memo to Europeans: Try washing your *whole* body; believe me, you'll smell better.)

P. J. O'ROURKE

The first kind of strange toilet the traveler needs to get used to is the squatter, which looks like Chief from *One Flew over the Cuckoo's Nest* just picked up the john, threw it out the window, and ran from the crime scene, leaving a six-inch diameter hole in the floor right where the toilet is supposed to be. The idea is that you are supposed to squat over the hole and, like a B-2 Bomber, hit the target. Managing this requires a number of skills, none of which fell within the scope of my liberal arts degree which, for lack of toilet paper, would have really come in handy.

DOUG LANSKY

In Istanbul, every restroom is guarded by a little old man sitting at a card table who charges you a minimum of 100 lire (about 15 cents) to use an open pit with no paper, no towels, no soap, and no deep breathing.

ERMA BOMBECK

The Japanese concept of "toilet" is basically the same as our concept of "a hole in the floor that somebody forgot to put a toilet on top of."

DAVE BARRY

FUN WITH LANGUAGES

American

One of the special beauties of America is that it is the only country in the
world where you are not advised to learn the language before entering. Before
I ever set out for the United States, I asked a friend if I should study
American. His answer was unequivocal. "On no account," he said. "The more
English you sound, the more likely you are to be believed."

QUENTIN CRISP

Chinese

When Coca-Cola first began selling in China, it was discovered that a literal
translation of the product's name into Chinese is "Bite the wax tadpole."

English

England is a country of many dialects.
Half the people don't know what the other half are saying half the time,
and wouldn't be on speaking terms with them if they did.

FRANCES DOUGLAS

The English have no respect for their language.
It is impossible for an Englishman to open his mouth without
making some other Englishman despise him.

GEORGE BERNARD SHAW

The devil take these people and their language! They take a dozen
monosyllabic words in their jaws, chew them, crunch them and spit them out

again, and call that speaking. Fortunately they are by nature fairly silent, and although they gaze at us open-mouthed, they spare us long conversations.

HEINRICH HEINE

To learn English, you must begin by thrusting the jaw forward, almost clenching the teeth, and practically immobilizing the lips. In this way the English produce the series of unpleasant little mews of which their language consists.

JOSÉ ORTEGA Y GASSET

One night in Rome, in the American bar of the Hotel de la Ville, I spoke, in English, with a Japanese businessman about America. He was from Hiroshima, but said he didn't hold that against me. He said in fact he was glad that Americans had occupied Japan because his people had learned much from our culture. However, he said, there was one thing about Americans . . . he searched for an example.

A colleague of his, he said, had been in America. Had penetrated so far as Ohio. And there, in a private home, this colleague "was served a sandwich of penis butter. "Penis butter?" Penis butter. I think it is an example of Protestantism and capitalism."

ROY BLOUNT, JR.

French

The American arrives in Paris with a few French phrases he has culled from a conversational guide or picked up from a friend who owns a beret.

FRED ALLEN

Paris is a great beauty. As such it possesses all the qualities that one finds in any other great beauty: Chic, sexiness, grandeur, arrogance, and the absolute inability and refusal to listen to reason. So if you are going there you would do well to remember this: No matter how politely and distinctly you ask a Parisian a question, he will persist in answering you in French.

FRAN LEBOWITZ

After dinner we felt like seeing such Parisian specialties as we might see without distressing exertion, so we sauntered through the brilliant streets and looked at the dainty trifles in variety stores and jewelry shops. Occasionally, merely for the pleasure of being cruel, we put unoffending Frenchmen on the rack with questions framed in the incomprehensible jargon of their native language, and while they writhed, we impaled them, we peppered them, we scarified them, with their own vile verbs and participles.

MARK TWAIN

The French, if you ask me, take undue advantage of the fact that so much of their language amounts to elaborate but probably indistinguishable variations on *ong*. I took French in high school and college, but in my experience if you try to speak it to a Frenchman whom you are not paying anything or whom you have already paid, he will look at you as if you are not speaking anything at all.

ROY BLOUNT, JR.

German

[The German language] was developed solely to afford the speaker the opportunity to spit at strangers under the guise of polite conversation.

National Lampoon

German is the most extravagantly ugly language.
It sounds like someone using a sick-bag on a 747.

WILLIAM RUSHTON

A verb has a hard time enough of it in this world when it's all together. It's downright inhuman to split it up. But that's just what those Germans do. They take part of a verb and put it down here, like a stake, and they take the other part of it and put it way over yonder like another stake, and between those two limits they just shovel in German.

MARK TWAIN

Like many European languages, German has formal (*Sie*) and informal (*du*) versions of "you." These were designed by Europeans primarily as a clever way to confuse American seventh-grade language students and thus keep the U.S. educational system lagging far behind their own.

There are no hard and fast rules for when one should use either version, but in general . . . you should *Sie* someone at least a few times before trying to *du* them.

CHRIS HARRIS

Hawaiian

"Aloha" is an all-purpose Hawaiian phrase meaning "hello," "good-bye," "I love you," and "I wish to decline the collision damage waiver." The Hawaiian language is quite unusual because when the original Polynesians came in their canoes, most of their consonants were washed overboard in a storm, and they arrived here with almost nothing but vowels. All the streets have names like Kal'ia'iou'amaa'aaa'eiou, and many street signs spontaneously generate new syllables during the night. This confuses the hell out of the tourists, who are easily identifiable because they're the only people wearing Hawaiian shirts.

DAVE BARRY

Italian

They spell it Vinci and pronounce it Vinchy; foreigners
always spell better than they pronounce.

MARK TWAIN

There is no Italian word for privacy.

PETER NICHOLS

Once in Bologna, out of desperation, I tried to have a chat with the stout
padrona of my *pension,* who happened to own a little Pekingese dog.
Although I could speak only two sentences in Italian—*"per favore, parla
inglese?"* and *"per favore, parla francese?"*—I thought to myself, the word
for dog in French is *chien;* and since Italian words are basically French words
with an "a" on the end, I pointed to the animal and said, *"cena?"* at which
point the woman's eyes bulged in horror as she grabbed the beast protec-
tively to her breast.

As I learned later, *cena* means dinner.

This was by no means the last of the mistakes I made in Italian; in fact,
ten years later, when I'd actually studied and begun to learn the language, I
started making even more. Once in Sestri Levante, for instance, my friend
Giovanna and her very correct Milanese parents and I were talking about the
various resort towns near Genova, one of which is called Chiavari. *"Ti piace
Chiavari?"* I asked Giovanna's mother, who went white. Later, Giovanna
explained to me that by mispronouncing *"Chiavari"* as *"chiavare,"* I had
asked her mother if she liked to fuck.

DAVID LEAVITT

Japanese

English Statement Made by Japanese Person	Actual Meaning in American
I see.	*No.*
Ah.	*No.*
Ah-hah.	*No.*
Yes.	*No.*
That is difficult.	*That is completely impossible.*
That is very interesting.	*That is the stupidest thing I ever heard.*
We will study your proposal.	*We will feed your proposal to a goat.*

DAVE BARRY

Latin

The Romans would never have had time to conquer the world
if they had been obliged to learn Latin first of all.

HEINRICH HEINE

Spanish

Frank Purdue's advertising slogan, "It takes a hard man to make a tender chicken," was translated into Spanish as "It takes a hard man to make a chicken aroused."

Language primers and phrase books for travelers can be an odd introduction to a foreign country. Blithely insensitive to the subtleties of polite conversation, these tiny manuals re-enforce the xenophobic notion that all foreign travel is rife with unpleasure and mishap. Sometimes the source of this unpleasure and mishap is unspecified—the reader of "Teach Yourself Catalan," for instance, can only wonder what dire circumstances will require the use of the phrase "I am prepared to raffle the goat."

HENRY ALFORD

Spanish is the language for lovers, Italian for singers, French for diplomats, German for horses, and English for geese.

SPANISH PROVERB

Vietnamese

Many languages in Asia are tonal. By adding a different inflection, or tone, to the same sound, it changes the meaning. Mandarin has four tones, Vietnamese seven. A young Vietnamese man attempted to teach me how to say, "No MSG please." He held his tact as long as possible, then busted a gut. The vocabulary was easy enough but apparently my English mouth was programmed to hit the tone to request "No boils on my ass, please."

JIM SOLISKI

WONDERS OF THE WORLD

Acropolis

Those who tiptoe around the Acropolis today in their thousands hardly
realize that they are looking at something like an empty barn.

LAWRENCE DURRELL

Alps

Such uncouth rocks, and such uncomely inhabitants!

HORACE WALPOLE

Blarney Stone

To get to it, you have to climb steep, narrow, tourist-infested steps
to the top of the castle; there, a local man holds you as you lean out over
the castle wall and kiss the Blarney Stone. Legend has it that
if you do this, you will give the man a tip.

DAVE BARRY

Broadway

What a glorious garden of wonders the lights of Broadway would be
to anyone lucky enough to be unable to read.

G. K. CHESTERTON

Eiffel Tower

Conceived by Gustave Eiffel to mark the hundreth anniversary of the
French Revolution at the Universal Exposition of 1889, the tower caused
nearly as much upheaval as the event it commemorated. Complaints
poured in as soon as the plans were announced. In an open letter of protest
to the director of the Exposition, three hundred of France's most prominent
artists and writers (one for each meter of the tower's proposed height)—
including Charles Gounod, Victorien Sardou, Alexandre Dumas fils, and
Sully Prudhomme—denounced the proposed tower as a "barbarous mass
overwhelming and humiliating all our monuments and belittling our works
of architecture." Others decried it "in the name of art and civilization."

This truly tragic street lamp.

LÉON BLOY

A half-built factory pipe, a carcass waiting to be fleshed out with freestone or
brick, a funnel-shaped grill, a hole-riddled suppository.

JORIS KARL HUYSMANS

This mast of iron gymnasium apparatus, incomplete, confused and deformed.

FRANÇOIS COPPÉE

This belfry skeleton.
PAUL VERLAIN

Guy de Maupassant, who eventually left Paris because of it, called the tower "a giant ungainly skeleton upon a base that looks built to carry a colossal monument of Cyclops, but which just peters out into a ridiculous thin shape like a factory chimney." Maupassant famously quipped that he liked to have lunch in the Eiffel Tower because it was the only place in town where he couldn't see it.

Despite the outcry, of course, the Eiffel Tower was erected and stands to this day on the Champs de Mars as the supreme icon of Paris. The tourists seem to like it.

Empire State Building

One thing I could never understand about the Empire State Building, why is it hundreds of people will come over from Jersey and pay a dollar to go up on the roof of the Empire State Building to look back at Jersey again.
FRED ALLEN

Golden Horn

I did not see the Golden Horn at Constantinople,
nor hear it blown, probably on account of the fog.
WILLIAM MAKEPEACE THACKERAY

Great Salt Lake

The largest inland body of salt water in the world, of no use, even for suicide.
CECIL ROBERTS

Leaning Tower of Pisa

Like most things connected in their first associations with school-books and school-time, it was too small. I felt it keenly.

CHARLES DICKENS

Malls

When you've seen one cluster of generic stores grouped under one management or one roof, you've seen a mall.

CHRISTOPHER HITCHENS

Mount Etna

I do not think I shall ever forget the sight of Etna at sunset; the mountain almost invisible in a blur of pastel gray, glowing on the top and then repeating its shape, as though reflected, in a wisp of gray smoke, with the whole horizon behind radiant with pink light, fading gently into a gray pastel sky. Nothing I have ever seen in Art or Nature was quite so revolting.

EVELYN WAUGH

The fatigue of ascending Etna is the only thing that has not been exaggerated in it.

SAMUEL TAYLOR COLERIDGE

Mount Everest

Everest is relatively easy to climb, given an experienced guide, porters, equipment and good weather. The result is that many inexperienced, well-heeled people climb it each year, a certain percentage die, and the mountain has become a leisure resort, albeit one dotted with corpses, turds and used oxygen cylinders, none of which decay at that altitude.

SEAN FRENCH

National Parks

The [national] park bears aren't what they used to be. . . . Most of the bears you see along the roads look as if they've spent the last five years squatted in a chair before a television set drinking beer and eating corn chips. Half of them should be in intensive care units. They have forgotten what it is that a bear is supposed to do. If panhandling along the roads were outlawed, they would probably hustle pool for a living. A dose of pure air would drop them like a shot through the heart from a .44 Magnum.

PATRICK F. McMANUS

Niagara Falls

Niagara Falls is simply a vast unnecessary amount of water going the wrong way and then falling over unnecessary rocks. . . . Every American bride is taken there, and the sight must be one of the earliest, if not the keenest disappointments of American married life.

OSCAR WILDE

Niagara Falls is very nice. It's like a large version of the old Bond sign on Times Square. I'm very glad I saw it, because from now on if I am asked whether I have seen Niagara Falls I can say yes, and be telling the truth for once.

JOHN STEINBECK

Pitch Lake

My conception of the pitch lake of Trinidad was formed in childhood and had been modified by no subsequent accession of knowledge. I had only to shut my eyes and murmur the words, "pitch lake of Trinidad," to see a black tarn, boiling hot, and surrounded by appalling precipices. My private pitch lake looked, in fact, like one of Doré's illustrations to the Inferno. Imagine, then, my disappointment with the real, the public pitch lake. For the real pitch lake is simply about two hundred asphalt tennis courts, in very bad condition, set in the midst of some gently undulating green meadows. I felt inclined to ask for my money back.

ALDOUS HUXLEY

Pyramids

The pyramids hustle is horizontally integrated. It begins with the cabbie, who happens to know the cheapest camel driver in all of Egypt, who happens to take tourists on a long detour to visit a boy on a burro selling Pepsis and papyrus, who happens to know a man with a Polaroid, who also happens to be an expert guide, offering, for an undisclosed sum, to reveal deep funeral chambers adorned with pharaonic graffiti. This last service was tempting. Ramses Loves Nefertari? Ozymandias Slept Here?

TONY HORWITZ

Its sole interest lies in its size. It is a simple-minded megalomaniac's dream come true. All the subtlety of engineering which went into its construction—the leveling of the ground, the dizzying calculus of stress and weight and proportion—was dedicated to a fantasy so crude that a human vegetable could have conceived it. It exists below the level of reason. Its contempt for money, labor, time, materials, its blind disregard of limitation or compromise, could be matched by any psychopath in a locked ward for the severely subnormal. All the Great Pyramid does is stand between you and the sun, like a mindless giant with his thumbs locked in his hip-pockets, saying, "OK?"

JONATHAN RABAN

The Pyramids, whose function as a public latrine no guide book mentions. . . .

V. S. NAIPAUL

St. Paul's

From the stone gallery there's a view
Of London that is simply heaven.
To see it, all you have to do
Is climb six hundred twenty-seven
Steps. It doesn't cost a penny.
The only thing is I found it exactly six hun-
dred and twenty-six steps too many.

PHYLLIS McGINLEY

St. Peter's

As a whole St. Peter's is fit for nothing but a ballroom,
and it is a little too gaudy even for that.

JOHN RUSKIN

Sistine Chapel

Business as usual: The slow, noisy shuffling of packed bodies as in a
stockyard whose animals are all looking to heaven.

ROBERT HUGHES

Stonehenge

Stonehenge nowadays is a zoo animal, an imposing but humbled beast,
captive behind a wire fence and a turnstile, embarrassed by the near
presence of a visitor's car park.

DAVID QUAMMEN

Sydney Opera House

The Sydney opera house looks like a typewriter full of oyster
shells . . . like a broken Pyrex casserole dish in a brown cardboard box.

CLIVE JAMES

Taj Mahal

An impressive pile built with public funds in Agra while famine scourged the
countryside. The Taj was commissioned by Shah Jahan to memorialize his
favorite wife, who died in 1631 giving birth to their fourteenth child. If Jahan
had really wanted to show his love, he could have cut back on the Viagra.

P. J. O'ROURKE

Takla Makan (Western China)

The Takla Makan, one of the world's largest deserts, has inspired
dread in merchants and travelers since the establishment of the Silk Road,
more than two thousand years ago: *Takla Makan* translates from
the Turkic as "You go in and you don't come out."

JEFFREY TAYLER

Vesuvius

Then on foot to Vesuvius. Monstrous mounting. Smoke; saw hardly anything.

JAMES BOSWELL

I don't have much interest in gazing upon volcanic mountains from afar—
I find it preferable only to gazing upon them up close.

CALVIN TRILLIN

Washington Monument

Saw Washington monument. Phallic. Appalling. A national catastrophe. . . .
Tiny doll-like people waiting to go into it.

ARNOLD BENNETT

White Cliffs of Dover

Crossing what the egocentric British like to call the English Channel is, as
everyone knows, a sickening experience, unrelieved by the sight of the white
cliffs of Dover which, in the pale moonlight, greet the nauseated traveler
like huge piles of slightly-off cottage cheese.

ALBERTO MANGUEL

Yellowstone Park

Yellowstone Park is no more representative of America than is Disneyland.

JOHN STEINBECK

THEME PARKS

The way tourism is now organized in America, it is assumed that travelers who want to see some calves roped and some broncos busted while in the West will take advantage of some efficiently packaged place with a name like RodeoLand USA, or maybe Cowboy Country. (Actually, it wouldn't be surprising to find RodeoLand USA in New Jersey—a Western wonderland plopped into the Jersey swamps to take advantage of what I sometimes call the Doctrine of Creative Inappropriateness. The Doctrine is based on the theory that tourists will stop in an ersatz Alpine town in Georgia not simply because they think it might be years before they get to Switzerland itself but because they treasure the notion of the gift shop clerk saying something like "I'm fixin' to show y'all some real nice *Lederhosen*.")

CALVIN TRILLIN

Disneyland

Disneyland is a white pioneer's idea of what America is.
Wacky American animals. American conviviality, zappy, zany, congenial
and nice, like a parade of demented, bright Shriners.

JONATHAN MILLER

Disney's California Adventure

Both times we visited, the park was deserted,
with workers standing around or, in one case, sitting around, doing nothing.
One was talking to another about her bad date the previous night, right in
front of the children. I wonder what Walt would say.

LESLIE N. HERSCHLER

Disney World

He knew he'd have to go to Disney World eventually. It's middle-class America's version of a pilgrimage to Mecca. Every family that can scrape up the cash must make the long and arduous journey to a shrine peopled with more minor deities than the slopes of Mount Olympus: Mickey, Donald, Huey, Louie, and Dewey. With frayed nerves and tattered wallets the faithful stream through the turnstiles of the Magic Kingdom, intent on giving every child his or her birthright: The opportunity to gawk at a six foot duck in a blue jacket.

CARYL RIVERS

Don't get me wrong. I like Disney World. The rest rooms are clean enough for neurosurgery, and the employees say things like, "Howdy, folks!" and actually seem to mean it. You wonder: Where do they get these people? My guess: 1952. I think old Walt realized, way back then, that there would eventually be a shortage of cheerful people, so he put all the residents of southwestern Nebraska into a giant freezer with a huge picture of Jiminy Cricket on the outside, and the corporation has been thawing them out as needed ever since.

DAVE BARRY

Visitors who care about real food will discover that gourmet dining is as much a fantasy as everything else in the Magic Kingdom.

Fodor's

Epcot Center

I realized that Walt Disney was a visionary. Some people have said that Epcot Center pavilions do not reflect the countries they're supposed to represent. This might be true—for now. But they will soon. And it's not going to happen by redesigning or reforming Epcot; the world is what's going to change. As twisted as this sounds, the world is already changing to fit Disney's crafted version of it. The Epcot Center is, unlike Tomorrowland or Future World, a self-fulfilling prophecy.

Countries around the world are now calling their historic treasures "attractions"; they make you buy a ticket and stand in line to see everything; nearly everyone speaks English (in order to sell the postcards, T-shirts, and trinkets); and one person in every tour group I've ever seen, from the Great Pyramids to the Great Palace in Bangkok, wears a Mickey Mouse T-shirt.

DOUG LANSKY

Euro Disneyland

A horror made up of cardboard, plastic and appalling colors,
a construction of hardened chewing gum and idiotic folklore taken straight
out of comic books that were written for obese Americans.

JEAN CAU

The prospect of the French running Disneyland sounded at first like one of those jokey "Trading Places" competitions run by magazines (John McEnroe to run a charm school, suggests F.K. of Surrey; Warren Beatty to be a monk for a day, says J.P. of Edinburgh).

MARK LAWSON

ON THE BEACH

The image of the beach is at once wholesome—healthy young surfers hanging ten, retrievers romping in the breakers, clambakes, volleyball . . . and the ideal romantic setting: Intertwined lovers rolling in the surf, famous shots of a wind-blown J.F.K. vigorously striding the sand (*pace* Nixon's clumsy attempt to appropriate the Kennedy magic with his own beach photo op, only to ruin it by wearing wingtips and a necktie). But what's the reality? Though ocean bathing and suntanning were once thought salubrious, maybe we need to rethink the whole beach experience.

Sunshine causes cancer. Parking is impossible, there are long lines for the rest rooms, and hot sand gets in everything. There are kelp flies, lugworms, sand fleas, tar, toxic spume, medical waste, oil spills, fish die-offs, red tides, riptides, jellyfish, and sharks. Fleets of cruise ships dump their garbage into the sea, and much of it eventually laps ashore. Beaches everywhere are routinely closed after heavy rains due to bacterial pollution from overflowing sewers, subjecting those hardy surfers to rashes, eye and ear infections, and stomach and respiratory diseases.

As for the celebrated glamour beaches of the world, the water at the Lido in Venice has been likened to hot saliva, Brazil's Ipanema and Copacabana are regularly declared unfit for swimming because of parasite-infested sea formations known as "black tongues," and body parts of murder victims regularly wash ashore along the Rio de Janeiro coastline. Florida's Key West, South Carolina's Myrtle Beach, and Puerto Rico's entire shoreline have all been cited for the poor quality of their beach water, and in Malibu, septic systems befoul Surfrider Beach and make Malibu Lagoon a fetid soup of fecal coliform and e-coli bacteria.

Surf's up!

As soon as he saw the red line on my foot he grabbed it to take a closer look. "*Bicho geografico,*" he said, "*sem duvida*" (without a doubt). He told me it was a parasite that burrows under the skin, penetrating too far to be cut out. As it moves around it leaves a red trail that makes your foot look like a road map. It had to be removed or . . . ? When I asked him the consequences of ignoring the critter, he shook his head at the unthinkable.

I had flashes of it eating its way merrily through my bloodstream and vital organs. I thought about the famous Brazilian *candiru,* the only known vertebrate parasite in the world. This small, slender fish lives on blood—any kind of blood. It usually enters the gills of the host fish and feeds on its blood, but has been known to enter the urogenital openings of human bathers, guided by the flow of urine if they happened to have peed in the water.

After forcing its way into the chosen crevice, it locks itself in place using the spines on its gill covers. Understandably, this causes excruciating pain and massive bleeding, often leading to infection. And you still have to figure out how to get rid of it. Surgery is often the only solution, and that's not a pretty thought.

ANDREW DRAFFEN

It is possible that future social historians will find it difficult to convince their readers that such a bizarre practice [as sunbathing] ever existed. Future generations may find the thought that the numerous ruined structures which they encounter over hundreds of miles of coastline were built purely in order that people could get their skin to turn brown no more intelligible than that the Great Pyramid was built to contain the remains of one Pharaoh.

JOHN CASEY

The prospect of a long day at the beach makes me panic. There is no harder work I can think of than taking myself off to somewhere pleasant, where I am forced to stay for hours and "have fun."

PHILLIP LOPATE

CABIN PRESSURE

If God had intended us to fly he would never have given us railways.
MICHAEL FLANDERS

I like terra firma—the more firma, the less terra.
GEORGE S. KAUFMAN

I don't like flying. The idea of my zip code changing every
seven seconds is too much for me.
TAYLOR NEGRON

When you think about flying, it's nuts really. Here you are at about 40,000
feet, screaming along at 700 miles an hour and you're sitting there drinking
Diet Pepsi and eating peanuts. It just doesn't make any sense.
DAVID LETTERMAN

I hate to fly, so I have a glass of champagne before I board and then
one on the plane, but I don't get drunk because I want to watch what's
happening. I try to read, but I find I'm riveted to the window, watching to
see if the wings are going up and down and trying to figure out how
the plane works, what keeps us in the sky.
MARTIN SCORSESE

I hate to fly. . . . Every time I get off a plane,
I view it as a failed suicide attempt.
BARRY SONNENFELD

I don't mind flying. I always pass out before the plane leaves the ground.
NAOMI CAMPBELL

I do not use airplanes. They strike me as unsporting.
You can have an automobile accident—and survive. You can be on
a sinking ship—and survive. You can be in an earthquake, fire, volcanic
eruption, tornado, what you will—and survive. But if your plane crashes,
you do not survive. And I say the heck with it.

ISAAC ASIMOV

If black boxes survive air crashes—why don't they make the
whole plane out of that stuff?

GEORGE CARLIN

I am not afraid of crashing, my secret is . . . just before we hit the ground,
I jump as high as I can.

BILL COSBY

The devil-airplane is responsible for, among other things,
cultural defilement (by taking certain people to places they were never
meant to be), loss of feeling for the true and awesome dimensions
of the country, and angel impersonation.

ANDREI CODRESCU

Airplanes have added nothing to our enjoyment of height. The human eye
still receives the most intense images when the observer's feet are planted on
the ground or on a building. The airplane belittles all it discloses.

EVELYN WAUGH

When it comes to flying, I am a nervous passenger but a
confident drinker and Valium-swallower.

MARTIN AMIS

There are only two emotions in a plane: boredom and terror.

ORSON WELLES

The wonderful thing about air travel today is that it gives people an idea of what it was like flying missions over Europe in World War II.

ART BUCHWALD

You nonchalantly ignore the safety demonstration, wondering why they still do the bit about life-jackets and inflatable rafts when no passenger plane in aviation history has successfully ditched in the ocean.

MARK LAWSON

If a passenger can't read the newspaper of the person seated in front of him, add another row.

BILL SAPORITO

If you want to fly somewhere, you must start by being herded—in and out, back and forth, up and down. First, you have to stand in line to get a boarding pass. That is to replace the ticket they just sold you. Then you have to stand in line to *show* your boarding pass. That is to prove you bought the ticket they just took away from you. This lets you stand in line to be checked for bombs. Next, you have to stand in line to give back the boarding pass they just gave you. (If you are flying in Europe, you will probably also have to show your passport here—for the third time.) This done, you get to stand in line to get on the plane, which enables you to stand in line to go down the plane. Eventually, you spot your place in the pen, jammed up against a window. But first you must stand in line one last time while this meathead in front of you takes an interminable time to arrange his trunk overhead. Finally, your way is clear. All you have to do is arrange your own trunk overhead. It won't take but a minute.

HENRY MINTZBERG

One did not "hop" on a plane. One took a long slow ride
to an airport, and argued for hours with ticket agents who seemed to
have been hired five minutes ago for what they supposed to be another job;
and if one survived that, one got to Chicago only to join a "stack" over
the airfield there, and then either died of boredom or crashed into
a plane that thought it was in the stack over Newark.

AMANDA CROSS

On my two-and-a-half-hour flight from Savannah, Georgia, to Newark, the
flight attendant made the following announcement: "The toilets are not
operational. If you must use the toilet, hold it until we get to Newark."

RENÉ CARILLO

Immediately after Orville Wright's historic 12-second flight,
his baggage could not be located.

S. HARRIS

I went to the airport. I had three pieces of luggage. I said that I want this piece
to go to Cleveland, this piece to Toronto, and this piece to Florida. The airline
agent said, "We can't do that." I replied, "Well, you did it last week."

HENNY YOUNGMAN

The scientific theory I like best is that the rings of Saturn are composed
entirely of lost airline luggage.

MARK RUSSELL

The first piece of luggage [to come off the carousel] belongs to no one.
It's just a dummy suitcase to give everyone hope.

ERMA BOMBECK

It costs $635 to ship a corpse one-way from New York to Los Angeles, but only $348 to fly round trip in coach. Now, what if halfway through the flight you die from eating the food?

JAY LENO

Flight Reservation Systems decide whether or not you exist. If your information isn't in their database, then you simply don't get to go anywhere.

ARTHUR MILLER

Air fares are now assigned by a machine called the Random Air Fare Generator, which is programmed to insure that on any given flight (1) no two people will pay the same fare, and (2) everybody will pay less than you. People are flying across the country for less than you paid for your six-week-old corn muffin at the airport snack bar.

DAVE BARRY

This is how the fare-war works: The various airlines announce bargain tickets for the same destination, which are sold out just as you get to the counter. You then have the choice of paying the regular fare or canceling the flight, which carries a penalty of five years in prison.

ART BUCHWALD

The food on the plane was fit for a king. "Here, King!"

HENNY YOUNGMAN

During [the flight] I ate a chicken breast so tepid that the cooking process could only have consisted of a stewardess breathing on it.

MARK LAWSON

I had the most expensive meal of my life today: Breakfast at the Airport.

ELAINE BOOSLER

What is airport food? We know it is priced inversely to the quality.
We know it looks as if it has been created in some central factory in Siberia.
And later, cramped like cranky sheep, we are stuck in seats
ridiculously small and given the same Siberian food.

MAIRA KALMAN

Do not accept any food from an airline that you would not accept from a
vendor in Calcutta. If it's bottled or if you peel it yourself, it may be all right.
Otherwise it may stay with you for the rest of your life.

ROY BLOUNT, JR.

Some airlines hire chef consultants. They correctly perceive the situation as
a public relations problem, but incorrectly believe that by attaching a chef's
name to a bad meal it will magically become a good one. Although chefs can
provide ingenious recipes, they cannot compensate for third-rate ingredi-
ents, precooking in stages, freezing and thawing, microwaving and reheating,
and cafeteria- and battlefieldlike conditions. Substitutions and shortcuts are
fine, but you still cannot make roast chicken without a chicken and an oven.

MARK BITTMAN

People who have never flown before love those little trays.
They are so adorable. The little cutlery, play knives and forks,
and everything tucked into everything else, plus a spot of appetizer
and a dash of dessert. Almost like real eating.

HENRY MINTZBERG

It's no coincidence that in no known language does the phrase
"As pretty as an airport" appear.

DOUGLAS ADAMS

Airports like abattoirs are white.

TODD MCEWEN

There's nothing like an airport for bringing you down to earth.

RICHARD GORDON

If one couldn't infer the hopeless middle-class-ness of airports from their special understanding of the ideas of *comfort, convenience,* and *lug-zhury,* one could from their pretentious language, especially the way they leap to designate themselves "International" or even, like Houston, "Intercontinental." They will do this on the slightest pretext, like having a plane take off now and then for Acapulco or Alberta, while remaining utterly uncontaminated by any sign of internationalism, like dealing in foreign currencies or speaking languages or sympathizing in any way with international styles.

PAUL FUSSELL

I landed at Orly Airport and discovered my luggage wasn't
on the same plane. My bags were finally traced to Israel where
they were opened and all my trousers were altered.

WOODY ALLEN

The limitless jet-lag purgatory of Immigration and Baggage at Heathrow.

MONICA DICKENS

Heathrow: The only building site to have its own airport.

ANONYMOUS

I sat in the Delhi airport and watched the big electric clock in the
departure hall that tells passengers when to board. I thought I imagined that
time was moving in fits and starts: 1:12 A.M. for fifteen minutes, then 1:27 for
another twenty, 1:47. . . . Closer inspection revealed that the clock was not
plugged in, and its digits were being flipped manually by a little man
in gray overalls whenever the mood took him.

JONAH BLANK

I had taken the Crossair flight from Lugano to Zurich, a tiny craft buffeted by Alpine winds, and then the Swissair jet to Kennedy. The food, wine and liqueurs in first class were very refined and they did not settle well. I was bloated with mineral water and yet had a sense of dehydration. This grew worse during the two-hour wait for immigration processing in a shed unconditioned against a very hot New York June. Some travelers fainted. A friendly Black wheeled round a tub of tepid water with paper cups. Immigration officers were inexorable in their checking of names against the great criminal ledger that looks like a variorum edition of Ayn Rand. They haggled over proposed length of stay and made shameless enquiries about solvency. I had ordered a limousine through my travel agent and was dehydrated further while waiting for it. It did not turn up, and the Swissair desk gave me a handful of dollars for a taxi. The driver was stoned and his cab reeked of old vomit. It was the New York rush hour and the driver's radio could easily have got through a Mahler symphony and two of Strauss's longer tone poems in the time it took to crawl from Queens to Manhattan. It was on loud and it played neither Strauss nor Mahler. When we reached the Marriott Marquis Hotel I knew I was going to die.

ANTHONY BURGESS

Given the fact that Los Angeles International Airport is the hub of a citywide transportation system that has no spokes, there is much about it to be admired. If you ignore the signs and run over the barriers, it's often relatively easy to find a parking space. The food court is a place over which Judge Wapner would be proud to preside. . . . The airport even has a new neighbor, an apartment building erected cheek by jowl with the northernmost runway, so that one could, if one chose, rent some rooms that offer the ultimate in noisy moving wallpaper.

HARRY SHEARER

The loudspeakers at [San Francisco] International airport are tuned perfectly: just high enough to catch your ear, just low enough so you can't quite catch the announcement.

HERB CAEN

He won't fly on the Balinese airline, Garuda, because he won't fly on any airline where the pilots believe in reincarnation.

SPALDING GRAY

It was 1977 and we were on an old DC-8 Air Ceylon coming in to Colombo, Ceylon, from Bangkok. The landing approach was pretty bumpy, but the biggest bump was saved for when we hit the tarmac—a massive shudder and shake—at least I hoped it was the runway. We were soon however airborne again and climbing steeply when a voice with a heavy Indian accent came over the PA as follows: I am sorry about the landing ladies and gentlemen, the pilot will now take over.

TIM STUART

Very few Mongolians can afford to fly, which is probably a blessing. The major domestic airline is called MIAT, which some wags claim stands for "Maybe I'll Arrive Today." MIAT uses aircraft that even Aeroflot has discarded, and the planes often lack toilets, air-conditioning, food or visible safety equipment. Expertise in the Mongolian Scramble is vital to buy a ticket, obtain a boarding card, have your baggage weighed, get to the door leading to the tarmac and find a seat on board (the number of tickets sold often exceeds the available seats). If you arrive safely—and at the correct destination—the Scramble starts again to get off the plane, find your luggage (if it hasn't been diverted to Bolivia or Yemen), plough through the throng of departing passengers and find transport into town.

PAUL GREENWAY

When Prince Philip stepped from an aircraft during a goodwill tour, a local official greeted him by asking, "And how was your flight, sir?" The prince replied with the question, "Have you ever flown?" "Yes, often," the man answered. "Well," said the prince, "It was like that."

I'll take three hours in the dentist's waiting room, with four cavities and an impacted wisdom tooth, in preference to fifteen minutes at any airport waiting for an aeroplane.

PATRICK CAMPBELL

After three hours on the ground, the captain of a Northwest flight from Chicago to Minneapolis told passengers that the flight had been canceled because the crew had exceeded their federally regulated time allotment for the flight.

A story among pilots, with a ring to it that is apocryphal but telling, deals with an airline nightmare called "the death spiral." A pilot brings a plane in very late, taxis to the gate and finds it occupied by another plane. The other plane is ready to push back, but can't because it is waiting for its crew. And who, asks the pilot waiting on the apron, is supposed to be on the plane at the gate? "Well," says the dispatcher, "you are."

MATTHEW L. WALD

La Guardia, the hellmouth of air transport. . . . If one drop of rain falls on La Guardia Airport, the cancellations are heard round the world.

GAIL COLLINS

La Guardia is my favorite airport in the world
because I like my runways as short as I can get 'em.

JERRY SEINFELD

It ought to be illegal for people to be in an airport if they aren't going
somewhere or coming from someplace.

ANDY ROONEY

There are people flying today who belong on Greyhound buses.

JAY LENO

Aeronautically [the flight] was a great success.
Socially, it left quite a bit to be desired.

NOËL COWARD

Beware of men on airplanes. The minute a man reaches thirty thousand feet, he immediately becomes consumed by distasteful sexual fantasies which involve doing uncomfortable things in those tiny toilets. These men should not be encouraged, their fantasies are sadly low-rent and unimaginative. Affect an aloof, cool demeanor as soon as any man tries to draw you out. Unless, of course, he's the pilot.

CYNTHIA HEIMEL

My wife and 6-year-old daughter were . . . bumped from a Continental flight from Flint, Michigan, to Newark. They were given $14 lunch money and put in a filthy van for a two-hour trip to Detroit to catch the next flight to Newark. On the way, the van driver decided to have breakfast; my wife and daughter sat in the McDonald's lot while he ate. The response from the Continental service representative was, "Well, we got them to Newark, so what's the problem?"

SAMUEL PARAB

Seated in business class on the interminable flight to Sydney, we were served the most unappetizing of meals, after which the cunning stewardesses—like those on any overseas flight—poured enormous cognacs, hoping they would knock us out for hours, and then disappeared and were extremely resentful when summoned for refills. One of the stews, however, did manage to endear herself to us, the naughty thing, by returning tippytoe in the wee morning hours to neck with the guy sitting in front of us.

MORDECAI RICHLER

Returning from a vacation in Bali aboard a packed Continental Airlines 747, the Beaulieu family of British Columbia were seated next to a patient in a hospital gown whose condition quickly deteriorated.

"I [saw] him choking and gagging and frothing and everything," said Donna Beaulieu. "His leg kept coming out into the aisle beside me. We were trying to push it back in so the food cart wouldn't run over it."

Three hours into the flight, the man died, but according to Mrs. Beaulieu, the flight crew virtually ignored the whole distressing ordeal and did little more than return the dead man's seat to the full upright position.

The Beaulieus filed a complaint with Continental for the trauma of being forced to sit next to a corpse.

I told my friend Mike the story about the man on the plane dying. Mike's a frequent flyer, and he said, "There are a lot of advantages to flying while dead."

"Like what?" I asked.

"Turbulence doesn't bother you, for one thing."

The Beaulieu family is seeking compensation for discomfort they endured during the flight. The discomfort ought to be worth beaucoup upgrades, huh?

The only reason anyone flies now is to get upgrades to first class. Nobody in first class would have cared if there were 10 stiffs up there with them—as long as they got the hot fudge sundae and the leg room.

Personally, I'd welcome flying next to a dead man. Next time I book a flight, I'm going to ask, "Got any dead guys on this flight?" It's like finding a mouse in your yogurt—or finding that glorious chicken head in your Hot Wings.

It's a gold mine. It's upgrades out the wazoo.

I'd kill to sit next to a dead man.

TONY KORNHEISER

You define a good flight by negatives: You didn't get hijacked, you didn't crash, you didn't throw up, you weren't late, you weren't nauseated by the food. So you are grateful.

PAUL THEROUX

There are only two reasons to sit in the back row of an airplane: Either you have diarrhea, or you're anxious to meet people who do.

HENRY KISSINGER

I was not prepared to do anything but upchuck and die after the eight-hour night flight from Miami on an Air Paraguay DC-8 older than most second wives that flew through the center of five Dr. Frankenstein-your-lab-is-on-the-phone lightning storms and aboard which I was served a dinner of roast softball in oleo.

P. J. O'ROURKE

In thirteen years as a flight attendant I've seen more than my fair share of air sickness. I once saw a drunken couple take turns barfing into each other's lap, as if playing a sickly version of "Can You Top That." I watched a Catholic priest vomit into the face of his secular seatmate. I watched a teenage girl open the seat-back pocket in front of her and proceed to fill it with the contents of her stomach. I watched a queasy businessman splatter the last row of passengers after an ill-fated sprint toward the lavatory.

In one particularly memorable episode that triggered a chain reaction of in-flight regurgitation, I watched the volcanic eruption of a 300-pound vacationer who'd eaten three servings of lasagna. After witnessing this spectacle (and inhaling the pungent odor that wafted through the cabin in its wake), more than two dozen passengers leaned into the aisle and retched. Gallons of heavy liquid splashed onto the carpet; even if you closed your eyes you could not escape the sound. Or the smell. I still get queasy just thinking about it.

ELLIOTT NEAL HESTER

The Federal Aviation Administration's 10-year, $12 billion program to upgrade the air traffic control system was a bust, and its software uses a 40-year-old language that's the computer equivalent of Etruscan. Plans are underway to modernize the software, but it will have to wait in line behind other important government priorities, such as ending global warming and reforming the Electoral College.

GAIL COLLINS

I'm fed up with it. I'm sick and tired of the delays, tired of waiting. I'm hanging it up. You can have it. This flight will be my last flight.

RAYMOND DAVIDSON, *Eastern Airlines pilot, who made the foregoing announcement to the passengers and crew, taxied his airliner back to the terminal at Atlanta's Hartsfield Airport, and walked off the plane.*

We took the Concorde back to London. It was three hours late in taking off, which nullified its one advantage over the old-fashioned jet.

ANTHONY BURGESS

Normal Barrett was flying to a Hawaiian island when he missed a connection in Honolulu because his United Airlines flight was late. As a result United offered him "alternative transportation," recalls Mr. Barrett, partner of a small real estate company in Waltham, Mass.

That turned out to be a charter flight on a commuter airline, which didn't bother Mr. Barrett until the plane—flying at night—had to abort its first landing; the pilots apparently had confused the parking lot lights with runway lights. On the second approach, the plane pulled up again—to avoid some workmen who were painting the runway, which had been temporarily closed.

"You could see these guys frantically waving their flashlights at us," said Mr. Barrett. "I was scared out of my mind."

Eventually, the flight landed at a nearby airport. But the terminal facilities were closed, so Mr. Barrett and five other passengers had to scale a wire fence to get out. A nearby hotel picked them up—and charged them $18.75 each for the van ride.

The Wall Street Journal, JANUARY 6, 1988

The conquest of the air, so jubilantly hailed by general opinion,
may turn out the most sinister event that ever befell us.

JOHN GALSWORTHY

MUST I GO DOWN
TO THE SEA AGAIN?

I shall never forget the one-fourth serious and three-fourths comical aston-ishment, with which, on the morning of the third of January eighteen-hundred-and-forty-two, I opened the door of, and put my head into, a "state-room" on board the *Britannia* steam-packet, twelve hundred tons burden per register, bound for Halifax and Boston, and carrying Her Majesty's mails.

That this state-room had been specially engaged for "Charles Dickens, Esquire, and Lady," was rendered sufficiently clear even to my scarred intel-lect by a very small manuscript announcing the fact, which was pinned on a very flat quilt, covering a very thin mattress, spread like a surgical plaster on a most inaccessible shelf. But that this was the state-room concerning which Charles Dickens, Esquire, and Lady, had held daily and nightly conferences for at least four months preceding: that this could by any possibility be that small snug chamber of the imagination, which Charles Dickens, Esquire, with the spirit of prophecy strong upon him, had always foretold would con-tain at least one little sofa, and which his lady, with a modest yet most mag-nificent sense of its limited dimensions, had from the first opined would not hold more than two enormous portmanteaus in some odd corner out of sight (portmanteaus which could now no more be got in at the door, not to say stowed away, than a giraffe could be persuaded or forced into a flower-pot): that this utterly impracticable, thoroughly hopeless, and profoundly prepos-terous box, had the remotest reference to, or connection with, those chaste and pretty, not to say gorgeous little bowers, sketched by a masterly hand, in the highly varnished lithographic plan hanging up in the agent's counting-house in the city of London: that this room of state, in short, could be any-thing but a pleasant fiction and cheerful jest of the captain's, invented and put in practice for the better relish and enjoyment of the real state-room presently to be disclosed:— these were truths which I really could not, for the moment, bring my mind at all to bear upon or comprehend. And I sat down upon a kind of horsehair slab, or perch, of which there were two within;

and looked, without any expression of countenance whatever, at some friends who had come on board with us and who were crushing their faces into all manner of shapes by endeavouring to squeeze them through the small doorway.

CHARLES DICKENS

"Spacious suites to enjoy as you cruise the Norwegian fjords." This is accompanied by a picture of a woman in an evening dress sitting at a small table while her husband in a tuxedo pours her a glass of champagne. What the picture doesn't indicate is that they have to hoist the table on the sofa before they can open the door, he is sitting on the toilet seat lid, the room is below the water line, the curtains cover a wall, and they are both trolls.

ERMA BOMBECK

Most piracy is of the mugging-at-sea variety. The pirates zip up in a speed-boat, point a rocket launcher at the hull and demand money. Lately it has been getting a little rougher. Last January, an Australian couple were sailing around the world. In the Gulf of Aden off Yemen, a small powerboat pulled up beside the couple's catamaran; a burst of machine-gun fire tore through the hull, wounding the wife. Four pirates boarded the boat, ripped out some high-tech communications equipment, then left.

Getting aboard a huge ship is easy if you have an expensive speedboat. But even the poorest fishermen know a simple tactic that is reported more frequently these days. Two sets of pirates get in two sampans and stretch a rope across a sea lane in the dark. When a big cargo vessel finally comes through, it catches the rope at the bow and neatly pulls the two boats right alongside. The pirates then heave up grappling irons, climb aboard and in the quiet of night clean the boat of everything portable. When they are finished, they just drop down to the boats and untie one of the lines. The sampans are immediately left in the ship's wake, and then they row back home, where a can of paint might fetch the equivalent of a week's pay.

Beats fishing.

JACK HITT

I would die of a cruise which is a super delight to vast numbers of travelers. It bores me even to think of such a trip, not that I mind luxury and lashings of delicious food and starting to drink at 11 A.M. with a glass of champagne to steady the stomach. But how about the organized jollity, the awful intimacy of tablemates, the endless walking round and round because you can't walk anywhere else, the claustrophobia?

MARTHA GELLHORN

A luxury liner is really just a bad play surrounded by water. It is a means of inducing hatred for your fellow men by trapping you in a confined space with too few of them to provide variety and too many to allow solitude.

CLIVE JAMES

Life on board a pleasure steamer violates every moral and physical condition of healthy life except fresh air. . . . It is a guzzling, lounging, gambling, dog's life. The only alternative to excitement is irritability.

GEORGE BERNARD SHAW

Boats are wretched. You see little but water, feel miserable and are condemned to whoever else was foolish enough to embark on one—generally the senile and very rich. It is no mystery to me at all why so many people commit suicide on boats. There's nothing preferable to do.

COLIN THUBRON

Going to sea, like going to Heaven, gives everyone a fresh start. The landlubberly past drops as swiftly from memory as the disappearing coastline. Social position ashore becomes meaningless in an autocracy where the captain represents, as occasion demands, the Queen, the Law, and the Established Church. Even clothes carry no distinction, one bikini or pair of shorts much resembling any other. Money is irrelevant, there being nothing to spend it on except gin and haircuts, both of which are very reasonable. A cruise ship is not a means of transport, but a comfortable, well-victualled desert island. Why people will pay heavily to involve themselves in such a primitive society is known only to deep-thinking anthropologists and the advertising executives of shipping lines.

RICHARD GORDON

I wondered why these passengers ever bothered to disembark, because all Greece was presented to them on the boat, albeit a Greece which existed nowhere else. In the lounge two dancers and a bouzouki band were putting on a performance of folk music. The dancers wore blue skirts and white blouses. As they twirled about, they looked at each other knowingly, with a twinkle in their eyes, as if this performance was a satire on the audience. They were not very good, if judged by the normal criteria of balance, rhythm, gracefulness, or unison. But perhaps in their own terms, they were excellent—high camp, did they think, or performance art? The audience, mostly Germans and Americans, had no way of knowing if this was how Greek dancing was meant to look, so they applauded with moderate enthusiasm. Afterwards one of the dancers took the microphone and sang "Strangers in the Night." It was my first encounter with Faux Travel, a fabrication designed to ensure that the consumer has all the comforts and no surprises.

DAVID DALE

We all like to see people seasick when we are not, ourselves. Playing whist by the cabin lamps when it is storming outside, is pleasant; walking the quarterdeck in the moonlight, is pleasant; smoking in the breezy foretop is pleasant, when one is not afraid to go up there; but these are all feeble and

commonplace compared with the joy of seeing people
suffering the miseries of seasickness.

MARK TWAIN

We . . . vomited as usual into the channel which divides
Albion from Gallia. Rivers are said to run blood after an engagement;
the Channel is discolored, I am sure, in a less elegant and less pernicious
way by English tourists going and coming.

SIDNEY SMITH

When John Masefield, the English Poet Laureate best known for such sea
ballads as "I Must Go Down to the Sea Again," arrived in New York after
crossing the Atlantic in an ocean liner, Mrs. Masefield told reporters, "It was
too uppy-downy, and Mr. Masefield was ill."

I know nothing so tedious and exasperating as that regular slap of the wilted
sails when the ship rises and falls with the slow breathing of the sleeping sea,
one greasy, brassy swell following another, slow, smooth, as the series of
Wordsworth's "Ecclesiastical Sonnets." Even immitigable at his best, Nep-
tune, in a *tête à tête,* has a way of repeating himself, an obtuseness to the *ne
quid nimis,* that is stupefying. It reminds me of organ music and my good
friend Sebastian Bach. A fugue or two will do very well; but a concert made
up of nothing else is altogether too epic for me. There is nothing so desper-
ately monotonous as the sea, and I no longer wonder at the cruelty of pirates.

JAMES RUSSELL LOWELL

I doubt whether anyone on land, who has never gone through with it, can
realize how time lags at sea. You may think you have seen a weary yawn, but
you have not, unless you have seen a man yawn on the deck of a ship after it
has been at sea seven or eight days. . . . There are the same passengers every

day, and the sea soon becomes as uninteresting as the wallpaper in a room you have lived in for months. I have heard about the changing lights and shadows on the ocean, but I have yet to see them.

E. W. HOWE

The sea is at its best at London, near midnight, when you are within the arms of a capacious chair, before a glowing fire, selecting phases of the voyages you will never make. It is wiser not to try to realize your dreams. There are no real dreams.

H. M. TOMLINSON

I have now seen sucrose beaches and water a very bright blue. I have seen an all-red leisure suit with flared lapels. I have smelled suntan lotion spread over 2,100 pounds of hot flesh. I have been addressed as "Mon" in three different nations. I have seen 500 upscale Americans dance the Electric Slide. I have seen sunsets that looked computer-enhanced. I have (very briefly) joined a conga line.

I have seen a lot of really big white ships. I have seen schools of little fish with fins that glow. I have seen and smelled all 145 cats inside the Ernest Hemingway residence in Key West, Florida. I now know the difference between straight bingo and Prize-O. I have seen fluorescent luggage and fluorescent sunglasses and fluorescent pince-nez and over twenty different makes of rubber thong. I have heard steel drums and eaten conch fritters and watched a woman in silver lamé projectile-vomit inside a glass elevator. I have pointed rhythmically at the ceiling to the two-four beat of the same disco music I hated pointing at the ceiling to in 1977.

DAVID FOSTER WALLACE

When does this place get to England?
BEA LILLIE, *aboard the* Queen Mary

GROUND TRANSPORTATION

Thanks to the Interstate Highway System, it is now possible to travel across the country from coast to coast without seeing anything.

CHARLES KURALT

I have the impression that all this
[the California freeway system]will end very badly.

CHARLES DE GAULLE

Europeans, like some Americans, drive on the right side of the road, except in England, where they drive on *both* sides of the road; Italy, where they drive on the sidewalk; and France, where if necessary they will follow you right into the hotel lobby. If you have a valid U.S. driver's license, you may drive in most European countries, but it's more efficient to simply leap off a cliff.

DAVE BARRY

By eight-thirty Paris is a terrible place for walking. There's too much traffic. A blue haze of uncombusted diesel hangs over every boulevard. I know Baron Haussmann made Paris a grand place to look at, but the man had no concept of traffic flow. At the Arc de Triomphe alone, thirteen roads come together. Can you imagine? I mean to say, here you have a city with the world's most pathologically aggressive drivers—drivers who in other circumstances would be given injections of Valium from syringes the sizes of bicycle pumps and confined to their beds with leather straps—and you give them an open space

where they can all try to go in any of thirteen directions at once. Is that asking for trouble or what?

BILL BRYSON

It is not true, as is often heard in Europe, that Sicilian drivers are unpredictable: They can be counted on to pass. On the highway, Sicilians pass on straightaways, they pass on hills, they pass on curvy hills and hilly curves. In a large city like Palermo or Catania or Messina, a traveler trapped in a motionless line of cars on a conventional two-lane street can suddenly find himself being passed on both the left and the right at the same time.

CALVIN TRILLIN

The only place one Sicilian will pass another Sicilian is on a curve. Occasionally a car or truck will be coming the other way and then the driver faces what is known in Sicily as "the moment of truth." If he swerves to avoid the oncoming car he will be considered a coward and his whole family will be in disgrace. He must force the other car to swerve. To see two brave men meeting face to face on a Sicilian highway is a sight one will never forget.

ART BUCHWALD

I was met at baggage claim by a guy named Samir. Samir warned me that drivers in Cairo are like no others anywhere in the world. I hear that everywhere I go though. Italians drivers are crazy, Russian drivers are crazy. Basically, everyone who gets behind the wheel thinks that everyone else is crazy. But after what I just saw, Samir was right. Most of the traffic lights just flash yellow. No one seems to pay attention to the lane markings. People drive between lanes and drift all over the road. People use their horns nonstop. Rarely was there more than a few inches between us and another car. It was like a stock car race.

HENRY ROLLINS

The horn is the one piece of Egyptian taxis that always works, long after the doors have rusted, the window levers have snapped off, and the meter has been hit with a hammer, or fed wooden slugs. Egyptians are also fond of driving at night without headlights, keeping them in reserve to use as a spare horn when a simple honk won't do. Honk-honk-flash-flash, honk-honk-flash-flash; they burrow like moles through the night.

Not surprisingly, Egyptian drivers are the most homicidal in the world, killing themselves and others at a rate twenty-five times that of drivers in America (and without the aid of alcohol). Motorists in other Arab countries are almost as driving-impaired. The only insight I ever gained into this suicidal abandon came from a speeding Kurdish driver, after he'd recklessly run over a bird.

"Allah wanted it dead," he said. The same fatalism applies to passengers.

Tony Horwitz

Driving in Africa is high adventure. It is impossible to tell what your driver or the driver of the car ahead—or behind—will, from moment to moment, decide to do: for no apparent reason any or all of these might take it into their heads to switch lanes; or stop without warning in the middle of the road to have a chat with a friend; or suddenly accelerate and overtake on an inside lane or a blind corner or steep rise where the oncoming traffic is an unknown quantity. (Pedestrians too are unpredictable. Without even a cursory glance to right or left, they will turn and walk calmly across the road.) The roadsides of East Africa are littered with the rusting remains of motorcars, buses and lorries. On a recent drive from Mombasa to Nairobi I counted no fewer than four freshly overturned lorries.

Shiva Naipaul

The only traffic laws [in Cambodia] are the laws of physics.

Patrick Symmes

I deciphered the system of extortion employed by [taxi] drivers plying the airport-midtown [Naples] circuit. They demand two or three times the fare registered on the meter, and should the victim protest, they offer a receipt that is four or five times what is on the meter. This way the driver cheats the passenger, the passenger cheats his company, and everybody prospers by participating in a satisfying life of petty crime.

ALAN RICHMAN

Cab drivers are living proof that practice does not make perfect.

HOWARD OGDEN

New York Taxi Rules:
1. Driver speaks no English.
2. Driver just got here two days ago from someplace like Senegal.
3. Driver hates you.

DAVE BARRY

I don't like buses. To ride a bus is to wonder how you're going to die. Is the bus going to break down? Is the driver going to run off a cliff? Is the guy in the next seat going to stab you? Are you going to get off the bus somewhere you shouldn't and never be heard from again? Think about it. Think of the form of transportation where there's the most mass death. Bus.

MARGO KAUFMAN

There is a reason for the multitude of religious symbols, slogans and prayers painted on Third World buses. Once they cram their doors shut and the wobbly wheels start forward, your life is in the hands of a supreme being.

ROBERT YOUNG PELTON

If you've ever flipped through your city's Foreign News section you've probably seen them: the Bus Plunge articles. Short articles about fatal accidents in countries with bad roads, steep mountains and heavy dependence on transportation by bus. Invariably, these articles begin with the words "A bus plunged . . ." and end with a quick count of the dead, usually numbering in the tens or dozens. They're terse, these Bus Plunge articles, and they always have terrible endings.

JENNIFER BREWER

If you anticipate a bus trip in Latin America, go through the following checklist prior to boarding:

Look at the tires. If three or more of the six tires (most buses include two rear sets of two each) are totally bald, the probability of a bus plunge increases. Visible threads on the tires means a blowout is imminent.

Does the bus have at least one windshield wiper? Good. If it's on the driver's side, so much the better. Try to avoid buses whose windshields are so crowded with decals, statues, and pictures that the driver has only a postcard-sized hole through which to see the future. Shrines to saints, pious homilies, boastful bumper stickers, and religious trinkets do not reflect the safety of a bus.

The driver's sobriety isn't a factor. The presence of his wife or girlfriend is. If she's along, she will sit immediately behind him, next to him, or on his lap. He will want to impress her with his daring at the wheel, but he will also go to great lengths not to injure her. If he has no girlfriend or wife, the chance of a gorge-dive increases.

You can't check the bus for brakes. Once I asked a driver in Guatemala about the brakes on his bus. "Look," he said, "the bus is stopped, isn't it? Then the brakes must work."

TOM MILLER

For most of the people who work in the city, the bus is the only means of transport, and the jams are not the only hazard. In Nairobi the bus crews work for rival companies, and they earn more money if they carry more passengers, so they race each other from one bus stop to the next. Sometimes rival buses, having raced side by side down a stretch of road, reach a crowd of passengers at the same time. The conductor and driver then fight each other, armed with crankshafts and wrenches and knives, to decide whose bus shall be filled to the point where any further passengers would fall off. In Kenya a single bus crash resulted in the death of ten passengers and the injuring of ninety-two others. After such a crash the police do not expect to interview the driver. If he is able to, he runs away and hides for some days.

PATRICK MARNHAM

The city bus tour: On one of these, you can sample the highlights of the city's traffic congestion, getting a terrific view of the entrances to some of Europe's most famous attractions. You will usually listen to a prerecorded history of these entrances on bus headphones that are precisely calibrated to always remain exactly ten minutes ahead of wherever your bus happens to be at the time. If you get bored, you can switch the channels and hear what static sounds like in other languages.

CHRIS HARRIS

The trick with these [Vietnamese] buses was not to sit at the back, because it would be full of chickens, ducks and catfish, and not to sit in the middle, because there was no room for your legs, and not to sit at the front, because it was absolutely terrifying.

JAMES FENTON

People in bus terminals look tired even before they start the trip.

JIMMY CANNON

The train? I'll take the train when a combination Orient Express and Bullet Train runs between New York and Los Angeles. But not until then, because contrary to the Amtrak ads in which gleaming, glass-domed observation cars glide through the Painted Desert, the typical view from an American train is of landfills, abandoned cars, propane tanks, and outhouses. The *backs* of outhouses.

HOWARD OGDEN

Rex Harrison's valet was killed while traveling by train from New York to Los Angeles to deliver his employer's hats. Harrison's reaction when he heard the news: "Now I suppose I won't get my hats."

Londoners are apologetic about their underground, which they believe has become filthy and noisy and dangerous, but which is in fact far more civilized than the average American wedding reception. At the height of rush hour, people on the London underground actually say "excuse me." Imagine what would happen if you tried an insane stunt like that on the New York City subway. The other passengers would take it as a sign of weakness, and there'd be a fight over who got to keep your ears as a trophy.

DAVE BARRY

What's the worst thing that can happen to you in an elevator? Mugging? Falling twenty floors to your death? Terrifying possibilities, but pale in comparison with what I believe to be every elevator rider's secret phobia: being stuck between floors, perhaps forever. Because of this fear, we have evolved precise, if unwritten, rules for behaving in an elevator. You must not speak to other passengers (except for quickly mumbled hellos), you must not establish eye contact, and you must face the door. This establishes an extreme impersonality, even a kind of invisibility, and this is precisely the attitude to have in a situation from which you cannot wait to be rescued. Establishing a relationship in an elevator would be tantamount to admitting that the fearful vehicle in which you are suspended is not a temporary aberration but perhaps a temporary home. Structurally an elevator car resembles both a jail cell and a burial vault; in order to deny these resemblances, we make ourselves deaf, dumb, and blind.

TAD TULEJA

How to Behave in an Elevator:
1. Face forward.
2. Fold hands in front.
3. Do not make eye contact.
4. Watch the numbers.
5. Don't talk to anyone you don't know.
6. Stop talking with anyone you do know when anyone
you don't know enters the elevator.
7. Avoid brushing bodies.

LAYNE LONGFELLOW

There's nothing about an elevator I like. It's filled with people I did not invite.
And often these people are wearing conflicting perfumes.

FRAN LEBOWITZ

BOOMER ON BOARD

Nothing has spread socialistic feeling in this country more than the use of the automobile . . . a picture of the arrogance of wealth, with all its independence and carelessness.

WOODROW WILSON

My casual disdain for SUVs went rabid one day not long ago while gassing up at a self-serve pump. I was minding my own business squeegeeing the windshield when the sun was suddenly blocked out by a seven-foot-high Ford Excursion bearing down on my midsize sedan. I shouted but it was too late. The driver could neither see me from her perch nor hear me over the blare of her stereo.

A fiftyish matron, she was in her own little luxury bubble. She clearly had no idea of the dimensions of her vehicle, because she cut too sharply while trying to round the pump island and clipped my front bumper, tearing it half off. With no apparent damage to her Excursion.

The impact having got her attention, she immediately pulled over, tumbled down to the ground, and calmly admitted fault, volunteering to pay for the damage "off insurance." She was so casual, so relaxed, so *agreeable*—she obviously knew the drill. Or maybe she was on Prozac.

The woman must spend a lot of time in gas stations because the Excursion, with its V-10 engine, averages under twelve miles per gallon. (When Ford announced plans to build the monster, the Sierra Club sponsored a "Name That Gas Guzzler" contest. The winner was a college student in Colorado who submitted "The Ford Valdez: Have You Driven a Tanker Lately?").

Good to her promise, the woman, or rather her husband's company, paid the repair bill (were they writing it off as a business expense?). They also dispatched not one but two secretaries in a taxi to escort me to the body shop ("travel and entertainment"?). The secretaries seemed to know the drill too. As far as I know, the woman is still cruising the neighborhood terrorizing other drivers.

My bumper may have been restored to its former condition, but I wasn't. I'd been radicalized, forced to the conclusion that something must be done about these wasteful, obscenely massive suburban assault vehicles, these wretchedly excessive luxury trucks, these *gasholes*.

Well, now I *can* fight back, thanks to Charles Dines and Robert Lind, two San Franciscans who describe themselves as "social activists" with the self-assigned mission to "stigmatize the insanity of mindless American consumerism and vapid status acquisition" represented by huge SUVs and, through negative publicity, change the SUV from a "status trinket" to a "badge of shame." Dines and Lind decry the wastefulness of a single commuter or mom on an errand to the local mall in a bloated behemoth, and call upon fellow citizens with a "sliver of conscience" to join their crusade.

"In the old days society had a pillory to shame people out of antisocial behavior," says Dines. "Today we have the mighty Bumper Sticker." Hence "Big Game SUV Hunting," tagging large SUVs with a specially created bumper sticker: "I'm Changing the Climate—Ask Me How." Stickers are available through their website, www.changingtheclimate.com.

CHANGINGTHECLIMATE'S RULES
AND GUIDELINES FOR SUCCESSFUL AND
ETHICAL BIG GAME SUV TAGGING

1. Only tag the big ones. The Ford Expeditions and Excursions (I avoid the Explorers), Chevy or GMC Suburbans, 1500's, 2500's which often go by the Yukon and Tahoe name. The Cadillac Escalade, Toyota Land Cruiser, Land and Range Rovers and Lexus LX470 are all to be considered targets of opportunity. It is best to tag in the affluent suburbs where you will notice the Urban Assault Vehicles are never dirty. I figure that most people in rural areas are probably using them for a functional purpose and therefore don't tag in these areas.

2. Do not tag small SUVs such as any Subaru, Toyota 4Runner, etc. Owners of these small and reasonably fuel-efficient SUVs keep complaining to me when they are tagged. We are after only the grotesque and bloated gas guzzling members of the SUV species.

3. Don't tag commercial vehicles, contractors, or any business affiliated vehicles. Also no pickup trucks. We have no gripe with people who really need these gas-guzzlers. It's the morons who are keeping up with the Jones' that raise my back hairs.

4. Don't retag vehicles that you recognize as already tagged (we can usually spot left over pieces from the original tagging).

5. We only tag late model vehicles, not some beat up old Suburban some poor soul has inherited.

6. Don't tag just because it's a four-wheel drive vehicle. Only the really big obnoxious ones.

With these restrictions there is still an unlimited number of eligible vehicles.

TRAVEL WRITING

Since the world watches the same television, wears the same clothes,
eats the same ethnic food and contrives to speak English,
who needs Murray or Baedeker?

SIMON JENKINS

The fat [Michelin] guidebooks keep offering the traveler to France their
expert opinions on which cathedrals to see, where to eat dinner, and how to
get the laundry done. In time, though, these volumes of authoritative
pronouncements can become oppressive.

OTTO FRIEDRICH

The letter with the foreign postmark that tells of good weather, pleasant
food and comfortable accommodation isn't nearly as much fun to read, or to
write, as the letter that tells of rotting chalets, dysentery and drizzle.

MARTIN AMIS

I know that life is an abyss, among other things, and like other travel writers,
I enjoy wire-walking a bit, courting, in a sense, catastrophe.

EDWARD HOAGLAND

I doubt whether I ever read any description of scenery which gave me
an idea of the place described.

ANTHONY TROLLOPE

Phrase books seem to be a universal and eternal source of hilarity and I think
I know why. Their authors go mad in the course of compiling them.

ALICE THOMAS ELLIS

Never trust anything you read in a travel article. Travel articles
appear in publications that sell large expensive advertisements to

tourism-related industries, and these industries do not wish to see articles with headlines like: Uruguay: don't bother.

DAVE BARRY

"April in Paris" inspired a friend of its composer, Vernon Duke, to visit Paris one April. Upon his return the traveler called Duke and complained bitterly about the constant rain and cold. Duke admitted that he never went to Paris in April precisely because of the foul weather, and that the original title of the song was "Paris in May," but the music required two syllables.

Books of travels will be good in proportion to what a man has previously in his mind; his knowing what to observe; his power of contrasting one mode of life with another. As the Spanish proverb says, "He who would bring home the wealth of the Indies, must carry the wealth of the Indies with him."

SAMUEL JOHNSON

I wish the novelists who write about the islands we are passing [in the South China Sea] would say a little more about the heat and perspiration, and a little less about the waving palms and the dusky queens.

ALFRED VISCOUNT NORTHCLIFFE

Just as tourism is not travel, the guidebook is not the travel book. The guidebook is to be carried along and to be consulted frequently for practical information. How many *rials* are you allowed to bring in? How expensive is that nice-looking hotel over there? The travel book, on the other hand, is seldom consulted during a trip. Rather, it is read either before or after, and at home, and perhaps most often by a reader who will never take the journey at all. Guidebooks belong to the world of journalism, and they date; travel books belong to literature, and they last. Guidebooks are not autobiographical but travel books are, and if the personality they reveal is too commonplace and un-eccentric, they will not be very readable.

PAUL FUSSELL

Most of what the American and Australian publics thought they knew about the isles of the Southwest Pacific had been invented by movie scriptwriters. Even as the Japanese were pictured as a blinky-eyed, toothy Gilbert and Sullivan race, so the South Seas was an exotic world where lazy breezes whispered in palm fronds, and Sadie Thompson seduced missionaries, and native girls dived for pearls wearing fitted sarongs, like Dorothy Lamour. In reality the proportions of the women were closer to those of duffel bags.

WILLIAM MANCHESTER

Those who write about the [Grand] Canyon generally begin by saying that it is indescribable, then they undertake to describe it.

JOSEPH WOOD KRUTCH

The Muses care so little for geography.

OSCAR WILDE

Syllables are always superior to sights.

JOHN ROBERT COLOMBO

TRAVEL GLOSSARY

air rage A catchall term for myriad forms of egregious behavior by airline passengers, caused by myriad forms of egregious behavior by airlines. According to studies, passengers are increasingly belligerent because of alcohol consumption, nicotine and oxygen deprivation, disruption of circadian rhythms, anxiety and fear of death inherent in air travel, separation from home and family, tedious security screenings, increasingly crowded conditions in airports and on flights, lack of respect for airline personnel, and thwarted expectations:

It wasn't supposed to be this way. We were told to expect medium-rare chateaubriand and exotic fondues and white linen antimacassars gentling our dreamy heads and fancy French wine all around and the bell ring of sterling flatware. These I was promised. Knifing through the jet stream at 50,000 feet, I would put up my stockinged feet, take my good wife's gloved hand, beam at our Cleaver-perfect children across the wide aisle and doze as we rocked safely into our future at 600 miles per hour. This is what we were sold. Promises were made, the ancient newsreel promises of commercial jet travel, circa 1960. The new magic carpet for the American leisure class.

Forty years later, we receive instead a $1,200 coach seat half the width of a human pelvis, a mismatched pair of circus peanuts and the in-flight director's recut of "Bicentennial Man." Behold, air rage.

JEFF MACGREGOR

airy No air-conditioning.

antitourist A tourist whose vanity and *tourist angst* compels him to distinguish himself from other tourists by shunning organized tours, consuming local food "no matter how nasty," eschewing the use of taxis in favor of public transportation, and ostentatiously not carrying a camera.

Sedulously avoiding the standard sights is probably the best method of disguising your tourism. In London one avoids Westminster Abbey and heads instead for the Earl of Burlington's eighteenth-century villa at Chiswick. In Venice one must walk by circuitous smelly back passages far out of one's way to avoid being seen in the Piazza San Marco. In Athens one disdains the Acropolis in favor of the eminence preferred by the locals, the Lycabettus. Each tourist center has its interdicted zone: In Rome you avoid the Spanish Steps and the Fontana de Trevi, in Paris the Deux Magots and the whole Boul' Mich area, in Nice the Promenade des Anglais, in Egypt with its excessively popular pyramids and sphinx. . . . But the anti-tourist deludes only himself. We are all tourists now, and there is no escape.

PAUL FUSSELL

black water Raw sewage released from cruise ships (cf., *gray water*).

carefree natives Indifferent service.

continental breakfast In Europe, croissants and coffee. In the United States, stale minipastries and Sanka.

controlled shore experience A *cruise ship* stop at a synthetic port of call such as Disney's Castaway Cay in the Bahamas or Royal Caribbean's Coco Cay, a 140-acre island where passengers snorkel in a lagoon containing a small plane that the company sank to give a sense of adventure.

cruise ship A floating hotel/amusement park/shopping mall (cf., *megaship*). "Cruising" is "tourism with a vengeance," according to Paul Fussell, who describes cruise ships as: "Small moveable pseudo-places making an endless transit between larger fixed pseudo-places. But even a cruise ship is preferable to a plane. It is healthier because you can exercise on it, and it is more romantic because you can copulate on it."

deluxe motor coach Bus.

direct flight A flight from point A to point B that may actually include stops at points C, D, and E (and/or a change of planes and/or airlines).

economy class Steerage.

economy class syndrome Also called "deep-vein thrombosis" or "DVT," a potentially fatal condition caused by immobility during long flights whereby a blood clot forms in a leg vein and travels rapidly to the heart or lungs.

ecotourism The dubious attempt to preserve wilderness by making it more accessible.

fare envy The sickening realization that your seatmate paid hundreds of dollars less for the same flight.

fare rage The ballistic form of *fare envy*.

frequent flyer A passenger enrolled in a program that awards bonuses, as upgrades or free flights, based either on distance traveled or on dollars spent using a special credit card.

Ever since the invention of frequent-flier miles, those insidiously addictive New Age green stamps, airlines have been at the vanguard of what are known in the marketing trade as "loyalty programs." Be true to us, and we'll be true to you. The airlines know what their customers forget, though: That such perks, in reality, aren't perks at all but accounting gimmicks priced into every ticket, and their psychological value far exceeds their economic worth.

WALTER KIRN

generica Standard features of the American landscape such as gas stations, strip malls, motel chains, and tract housing that are virtually identical all over the country.

gentle breezes Typhoons.

gray water Wastewater from sinks, showers, and washing machines released by cruise ships (cf., *black water*).

living history Tourist attractions featuring costumed role-players reenacting historical events or milieux, as at Greenfield Village, Michigan; Mystic Seaport, Connecticut; and Colonial Williamsburg, Virginia:

Colonial Williamsburg, which more or less invented the "living history" phenomenon in the 1930s, has long been accused of glossing over the realities of slavery in 18th-century Virginia. So a couple of years ago, the park began staging true-to-life depictions of runaway-slave patrols and whippings, using African-American and white "interpreters." Children were terrified, and on at least one occasion, adult members of the audience attacked the white actors in the slave patrol, trying to wrest away their fake muskets.

ADAM GOODHEART

megaship The latest generation of *cruise ship* such as Carnival Cruise Line's "funship" *Destiny,* which Carnival claims to be "the most successful ship since the Ark." Built at a cost of $400 million, *Destiny* is twice the size of the *Titanic* and routinely carries three thousand "guests" (not "passengers") and one thousand in crew on weeklong Caribbean cruises. With its nine-deck-high atrium and glass elevators, it is too big to pass through the Panama Canal.

Princess Cruises's *Grand Princess* is slightly smaller (twenty-six hundred passengers) than *Destiny* but cost more to build ($450 million). Taller than Niagara Falls, the *Grand Princess* has an eight-hundred-seat theater, twelve cocktail lounges, seven restaurants, three grand dining rooms, a juice bar, a spa, swimming pools, tennis courts, a jogging track, a putting green, and a wedding chapel.

Megaship activities include nightclubbing, karaoke, casino gambling, bingo, dance lessons, weight-loss seminars (despite plentiful food and frequent feedings), art auctions, wine-tastings, hairy-chest contests, and even shuffleboard.

midair passenger exchange An air-traffic-controller euphemism for a head-on collision, an event immediately followed by "aluminum rain."

minthead A condition caused by going to bed in your hotel room without noticing the chocolate mint on your pillow.

There was . . . a gold-wrapped chocolate on each pillow, it being a peculiar assumption of expensive hotels that the kind of people who can afford to pay a laborer's weekly wage for one night's accommodation will suddenly go ape-shit with gratitude for a free piece of confectionery.

MARK LAWSON

---

mordida Aka "baksheesh," "dash," "local tax." A bribe to secure a service that would be free at home, for example, the issuance of visas, the right of passage on highways. Also, on-the-spot "fines" for minor infractions, real or contrived.

Love it or hate it, baksheesh is a way of life in Egypt. Almost everyone wants largesse in exchange for a service, even one as small as turning on a washroom tap. And, everyone has a favorite story.

My award for sheer gall goes to an old guy hanging around the Pyramids, who mooched a cigarette off me . . . then demanded baksheesh in return for lighting mine! But, as a practitioner of the art, he's left a country mile behind the mounted policeman I met at the Citadel.

Sitting on a beautiful white horse, sternly moustached, dressed in immaculate whites, and caparisoned in *aiguillettes* and shining black leather, he was a picture waiting to be taken. *"Moomkin surah?"* (May I take a picture?) I asked. *"Inshallah!"* said the magnificent representative of Cairo's Finest, nodding in agreement.

God was indeed willing; I took my pictures and felt in my pocket for a small note for the customary "model fee." "No! No!" said the policeman, shaking his head. "Policemans must not take baksheesh!" Then he reached down, took the note and grinned. "Horse can take baksheesh!!"

KEITH KELLETT

oceanfront Damp and noisy.

ocean view You can see the ocean from your room. You just can't get to the ocean from your hotel.

old world charm No running water.

open jaw A round trip in which the passenger returns to a place other than the point of origin. Not coincidentally, a term also applied to oral surgery.

orientation tour Drive-by sightseeing.

people eater An apt nickname for "jetway," the airless maw through which passengers are fed into, and disgorged from, airliners.

> Never trust anything you read in a travel article. If a travel article describes the native denizens of a particular country as "reserved," this means that when you ask them for directions, they spit on your rental car.
>
> DAVE BARRY

quaint No indoor plumbing.

recently renovated They'll be hammering in the next room.

reentry Psychologists studying problems involved in returning from vacation have found that any stress-reducing benefits of a holiday are quickly erased by the trauma of going back to work. The incidence of heart attacks is higher on Monday mornings, and even higher on Monday mornings immediately after a vacation.

It stands to reason that an enjoyable trip might lead to an emotional hangover, but studies indicate that *reentry* is even more difficult for people whose vacations were disappointing.

We usually think of a vacation as a stratagem to divert your brain with new sights and tastes (a "change"). The idea is to shed the worries of your life and restore your energy to face them again. I wonder, though, if that is often the result. The vacation I remember most was the one during which I realized I wanted to kill my husband.

He was standing with his back to me, gazing into a magnificent and deep canyon in Utah, and it came to me that if I were to hurl myself at him with all my force, precipitating him thousands of feet into the chasm, my troubles would be over. Only then did I begin to suspect that all was not right in my life. Vacations sometimes provide the leisure to realize unpleasant things you haven't had time to notice before, and maybe it's this that makes it so hard for almost everybody to come home to face real life again.

DIANE JOHNSON

runway rage A subspecies of *air rage* occasioned by long takeoff delays. On one flight from Newark to Chicago, coach passengers found themselves sitting on the runway for several hours, first smelling the food being served in first class, later smelling the overflowing toilets. When the plane finally received clearance, it was too low on fuel to take off.

secluded You can't get there from here.

tourist angst According to the British journalist Alan Brien, the gnawing fear that you're a tourist just like everyone else. See also, *antitourist*.

tropical Rainy.

INDEX

ABOUT THE AUTHOR

Jon Winokur, author of the best-selling *Portable Curmudgeon,* lives in Pacific Palisades, California. He has traveled extensively throughout western Los Angeles.

SASQUATCH BOOKS
www.sasquatchbooks.com